Handmade Books
for Everyday Adventures

Also by Erin Zamrzla

At Home with Handmade Books: 28 Extraordinary Bookbinding
Projects Made from Ordinary and Repurposed Materials

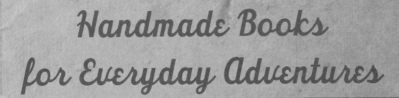

Handmade Books for Everyday Adventures

20 Bookbinding Projects for Explorers, Travelers, and Nature Lovers

Erin Zamrzla

ROOST BOOKS

Boston & London
2013

Roost Books
An imprint of Shambhala Publications, Inc.
Horticultural Hall
300 Massachusetts Avenue
Boston, Massachusetts 02115
roostbooks.com

9 8 7 6 5 4 3 2 1

First Edition
Printed in China

⊗ This edition is printed on acid-free paper that meets the American National Standards Institute Z39.48 Standard.
♻ Shambhala makes every effort to print on recycled paper.
For more information please visit www.shambhala.com.

Distributed in the United States by Random House, Inc.,
and in Canada by Random House of Canada Ltd

Designed by Katrina Noble

Library of Congress Cataloging-in-Publication Data

Zamrzla, Erin.
Handmade books for everyday adventures: 20 bookbinding projects for explorers, travelers, and nature lovers / Erin Zamrzla.—First edition.
Pages   cm
Includes bibliographical references.
ISBN 978-1-61180-008-1
1. Bookbinding—Handbooks, manuals, etc. 2. Nature craft. I. Title.
Z271.Z363 2013
686.3'02—dc23
2012049002

Special thanks to Mom for sharing so many great ideas, resources, photography props, and encouragement. My most sincere thanks to Ben for working alongside me the entire way. I couldn't have done it without you.

Contents

Introduction

I always carry a book and pen with me, as I never know when inspiration will strike. When I create a new handmade book, I often consider how well it will travel with me on my daily journeys. Think of all the places you go, day in and day out. How often do you jot notes, make lists, write, journal, sketch, or draw?

The projects in this book are designed to bring along with you on your day-to-day adventures. Not only will you find unique places to journal and sketch, but you will discover projects to join you just about anywhere you may go.

Bookbinding is a versatile craft; for me, it combines my love of paper and interesting materials with functional projects. Traditional Japanese bookbinding forms the basis for the projects within these pages. You will find several variations of historical stab bindings and accordion folds.

The Japanese four-hole, noble, hemp-leaf, and tortoise-shell bindings hold together pages and covers through holes that penetrate all the way through a book. This is why they are often called stab bindings. The stitching patterns are flexible and leave room for experimentation. You can adapt them to all book sizes and a variety of materials. The Yamato and account book bindings also stitch through the entire thickness of a book. Account books traditionally have long strings that extend off the binding and can be used to hang your book wherever you like. Ledger books are not stab bound but are sewn along the fold of pages folded in half. They are quick and easy to make.

The pages of accordion and flutter books are created from a long strip of paper folded back and forth until it is just the right size to fit inside the cover. The only difference between the two bindings is the cover; accordion books are sandwiched between two separate covers, while the cover of a flutter book is constructed of one piece and wraps around the spine.

The only nontraditional binding included among the projects is the glue binding. This simple binding can be used as an inner binding to hold the pages of a book together before attaching the covers with a decorative stab binding.

I took the liberty to update and adapt the traditional bindings for use with modern materials. I encourage the creative use of recycled materials and materials that you already have.

The projects in this book vary from basic to advanced. If you have never tried bookbinding before, this is a great place to start. If you are already familiar with these bindings, you will still find unique and challenging projects to create.

There are many places to go and many new things to try. Why not start by creating a handmade book to bring with you on your next adventure?

Everyday Outings

Create a book to record your daily thoughts, make lists, send notes of encouragement, or even to wear. These projects are the perfect companions to your everyday outings.

Grocery List Pad

carrots
strawberries
~~turnip~~
~~cucumber~~
bell pepper
tomatoes
eggs
cherries

This simple pad is easy to make and is a great way to recycle scraps of unused paper. Add a magnet to the back and hang it on the fridge for easy access. You can easily remove the pages as needed.

Finished Size

4" × 6"

Tools

Metal ruler

Craft knife

Cutting mat or protective cutting surface

Bulldog clips

Waxed paper

PVA (white glue) (allow to sit out for a few minutes to thicken)

Small glue brush

Materials

Text weight paper: 50 pages, each 4" wide and up to 6" in length

Chip board: 1 piece, 4" × 6"

Adhesive magnetic strip: 1 piece, 3 ½" × ½"

Instructions

1. Trim your papers to size with a metal ruler and craft knife.

2. Arrange the text weight pages in order with the longest pages on the bottom and the shortest pages on the top.

3. Place the chip board at the bottom of the stack of pages. Align the chip board and pages at the spine and clip them with a bulldog clip on each side, near the spine but not touching the spine. Place a small piece of scrap paper between the clip and the pages to prevent the clip from damaging the pages.

4. Lay the pad flat on a piece of waxed paper. Slide the spine of the book just off of the edge of your work surface. Brush on a layer of PVA along the spine. Let the glue dry completely. Repeat, building up three or four coats of glue.

5. Remove the clips and adhere the magnetic strip to the back of the pad, near the top.

6. Hang the list pad on a refrigerator or other metal surface.

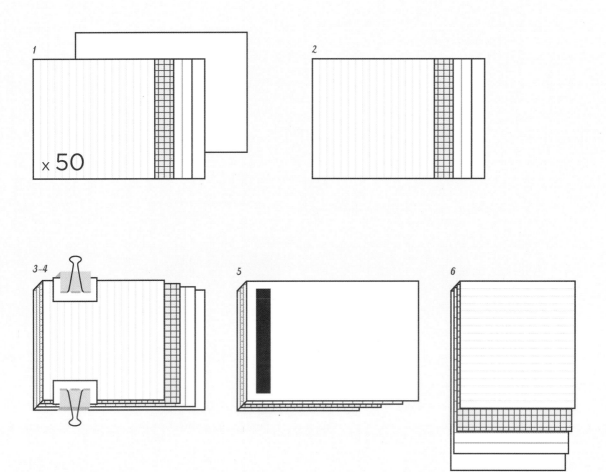

Lunch Box Notes

Fill the pages of this book with cheerful notes of encouragement. Simply remove a perforated page to include in the lunch box or briefcase of someone you care about. The pages can be pre-printed or left blank for writing a note as needed. A shape punched into the front cover reveals a colorful patterned paper behind.

Finished Size

4 ¼" × 2 ¾"

Tools

Metal ruler

Craft knife

Cutting mat or protective cutting surface

Computer and printer (optional)

Rotary perforator

Bone folder

Craft punch

Pencil

Bulldog clip

Awl or small hole punch

Tapestry or binder's needle

Scissors

Materials

Text weight paper: 20–40 pages, each 4 ¼" × 2 ¾"

Card stock: 2 pieces, each 4 ¼" × 2 ¾"

Liner paper: 4 ¼" × 2 ¾"

Template paper: 4 ¼" × 2 ¾"

Kitchen twine: 15"

Instructions

1. Trim your papers to size with a metal ruler and craft knife. If you plan to include handwritten notes on the pages, cut your text weight paper to size. If you plan to print the notes from a computer, wait to cut your text weight paper to size.

2. To print a note on each inside page, divide an 8 ½" × 11" page into eight equal parts, each 4 ¼" × 2 ¾". Type a message in each of the eight parts and print out three to five pages.

3. Cut the 8 ½" × 11" pages into eight smaller pages, each 4 ¼" × 2 ¾".

4. Working one page at a time, use a rotary perforator to perforate each inside page ½" from the spine edge.

5. Use a ruler and bone folder to score the front cover ½" from the spine edge.

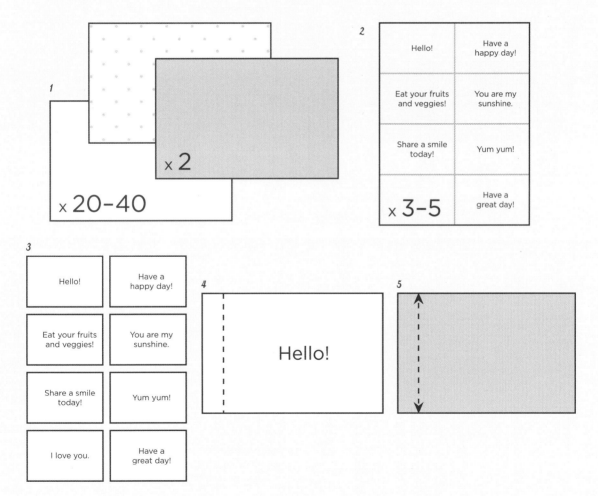

6. Use a craft punch to punch a shape from the center of the front cover.

7. Use a ruler and bone folder to score the liner paper ½" from the spine edge.

8. Cut a piece of scrap paper to size to serve as a hole punch template. Mark a line ¼" from the spine edge. Mark two holes along this line, evenly distributed between the edges of the page.

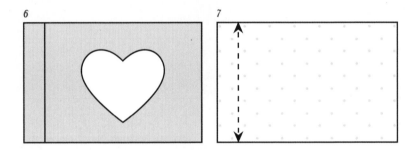

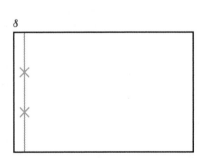

9. Arrange your papers in order: back cover, inside pages, front liner paper, and front cover. Clip with a bulldog clip along the fore edge. Place a small scrap of paper between the clip and the pages to prevent the clip from damaging the pages.

10. Use the template to punch holes through the entire thickness at the spine. A ⅛" hole punch will accommodate the thickness of your kitchen twine.

11. Stitch the spine following the instructions for the Yamato binding on pages 186–87.

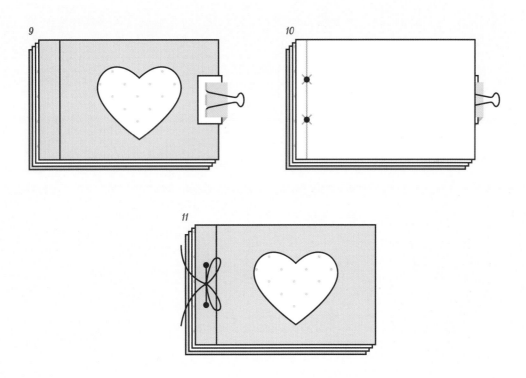

Necklace Book

Take notes on the tiny pages of this wearable book. Coated jewelry wire holds together a pretty cover and blank pages and extends to serve as a necklace. Make several, and you can wear a different one every day of the week.

Finished Size

1" × 1 ½" × ¼"

Tools

Metal ruler

Craft knife

Cutting mat or protective cutting surface

Pencil

Bulldog clip

Awl

Small hole punch or 2mm Japanese screw punch

Scissors

Materials

Medium weight paper: 30 pages, each 1" × 1 ½"

Hole punch template: 1" × 1 ½"

Book cloth or thin leather for cover: 1" × 3 ½"

Decorative liner paper: 1" × 3 ½"

Nylon coated bead stringing wire: 2 strands, each 36"

Instructions

1. Trim your materials to size with a metal ruler and craft knife. Make sure that the grain of each paper is parallel to the short side.

2. Create a hole punch template. Mark a line ³⁄₁₆" from the spine edge. Mark two holes along this line, evenly distributed between the edges of the page.

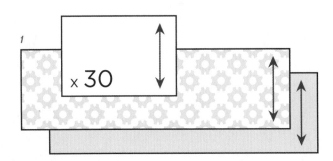

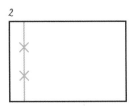

3. Carefully line up the pages and clip with a bulldog clip at the fore edge. Place a small piece of scrap paper between the clip and the pages to prevent the clip from damaging the pages.

4. Line up the template at the spine and punch holes in the stack of pages at the marks.

5. Place the cover piece on top of the liner paper, both facing up. Wrap the liner and cover together over the spine of the pages so that a small amount extends past the pages at both the front and back.

6. To mark the holes for the cover and liner paper, lay the cover and pages on a cutting mat with the cover still wrapped around the spine of the pages. Lift up the front cover and poke an awl down through the existing holes in the pages and through the back cover and liner paper.

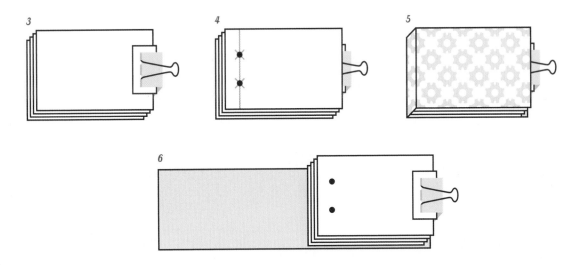

7. Lay the front cover back in place, hold the cover and pages firmly together, and flip over. Lift up the back cover and repeat, marking the front cover and liner paper.

8. Remove the cover and liner paper and lay flat on a cutting mat. Punch through both layers at all four marks with a small hole punch or 2mm Japanese screw punch.

9. Place the punched cover and liner paper over the clipped pages.

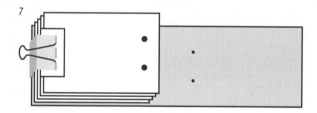

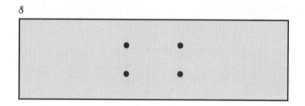

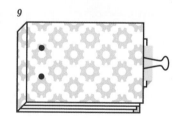

10. Stitch the spine following the instructions for the account book binding on pages 188–91. If your holes are large enough, you won't need a needle and can stitch with the wire alone.

11. Tie the wires together at the end so that your necklace is the desired length. Trim any excess wire.

12. Remove the bulldog clip and use a metal ruler and craft knife to trim excess cover and liner paper that extends past the fore edge of the pages.

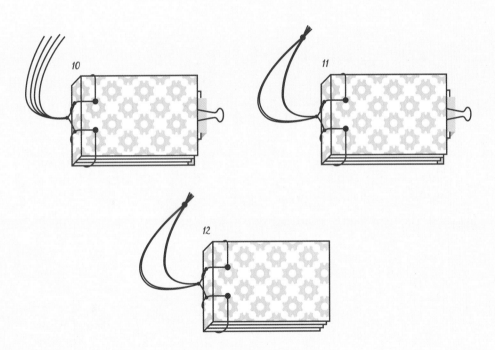

Cross Stitch Cover

The front cover of this book is created from cross stitch canvas and is intentionally left blank as a work-in-progress. Bring it along on your next outing to occupy time, either by stitching on the covers or writing inside.

Finished Size

8 ¼" × 5 ½" × ⅜"

Tools

Metal ruler

Craft knife

Cutting mat or protective cutting surface

Fabric scissors or rotary cutter

Pencil

Bulldog clip

Awl or Japanese screw punch

Tapestry or binder's needle

Materials

Plastic cross stitch canvas: 2 pieces, each 8 ¼" × 5 ½" (this is equal to a single sheet cut in half)

Felt: 2 pieces, each 8 ¼" × 5 ½"

Text or drawing weight paper: 20–30 pages, each 8 ¼" × 5 ½"

Template paper: 8 ¼" × 5 ½"

Embroidery floss: 35"

Instructions

1. Trim your plastic canvas and paper to size with a metal ruler and craft knife. Trim your felt to size with fabric scissors or a metal ruler and rotary cutter.

2. Cut a piece of scrap paper to size to serve as a hole punch template. Mark two lines, one ⅜" from the spine edge and another ³⁄₁₆" from the spine edge. Mark four holes along the inner line, one ⅝" from the top, another ⅝" from the bottom, and the third and fourth evenly distributed between the first two holes. Mark two holes along the outer line, one ⁵⁄₁₆" from the top, and the second ⁵⁄₁₆" from the bottom.

3. Carefully line up the inside pages and clip with a bulldog clip at the fore edge. Place a small piece of scrap paper between the clip and the pages to prevent the clip from damaging the pages.

4. Align the template along the spine and punch holes in the pages at the marks.

5. Working one cover at a time, align the template along the spine and punch holes at the marks with an awl or Japanese screw punch.

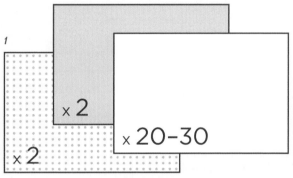

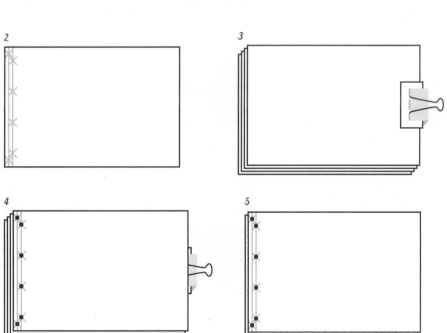

6. Working with one piece of felt at a time, align the template along the spine and punch holes at the marks with an awl or Japanese screw punch.

7. Place the materials in order: plastic canvas on bottom, felt, pages, felt, and plastic canvas on top. You may wish to clip the entire thickness together with a bulldog clip before stitching.

6

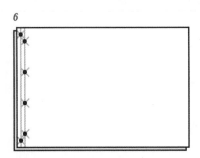

7

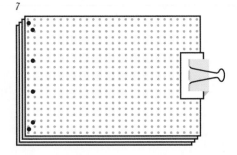

8. Stitch the spine following the instructions for the noble binding on pages 158–63.

9. After your book is complete, follow a favorite cross stitch pattern to stitch onto the front and back covers. After stitching, sew the felt to the back side of each cover to hide the back, if desired.

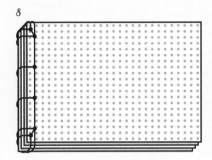
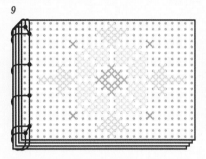

Write Your Own Story Journal

Wherever you may wander, be sure to bring along this journal to record your thoughts. The accordion-folded pages tuck into a wraparound cover. Choose to make a flexible softcover version or create a sturdy hardcover version.

SOFTCOVER INSTRUCTIONS

Finished Size

5 7/8" × 9" × 5/16"

Tools

Metal ruler

Craft knife

Cutting mat or protective cutting surface

Pencil

Bone folder

Bulldog clip

Waxed paper

Paste, glue, or glue stick

Small paste brush (if using paste or glue)

Book press or heavy stack of books

Materials

Drawing paper (medium weight): 10 pieces, each 12" × 9"

Decorative paper for cover: 1 piece, 14" × 11"

Drawing paper (to reinforce the cover): 1 piece, 11 7/8" × 9"

Instructions

1. Trim your papers to size with a metal ruler and craft knife.

2. Use a ruler and bone folder to score along the length of each inside page ½" from the left edge.

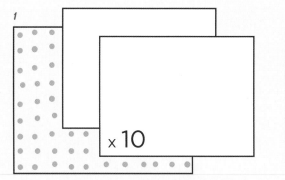
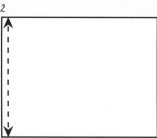

3. Fold each ½" flap to the back of the page. Burnish.

4. With the flap folded under, fold the remaining page in half, right to left. Burnish. Repeat, folding all inside pages in half.

5. Stack the folded pages with the folded flaps facing the same direction. Clip with a bulldog clip at the opposite side, away from the flaps. Place a small piece of scrap paper between the clip and the pages to prevent the clip from damaging the pages.

6. Lay the stack of pages with the top flap facing up. Starting at the bottom of the stack, tuck a small piece of waxed paper under a flap and apply paste to the flap. Adhere it to the next page. Repeat until all pages are connected. Press until dry.

7. Lay out the decorative cover paper face down. Use a ruler and bone folder to score along the length of the decorative cover paper 1" from the top and 1" from the bottom.

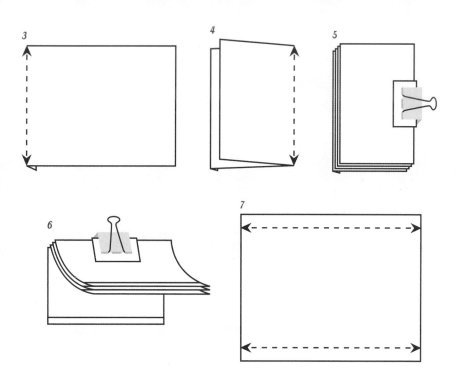

8. Fold over the top and bottom edges to the inside so that the cover is the same height as the inside pages. Burnish.

9. With the cover paper still face down, use a ruler and bone folder to score along the left side 1" from the edge. Fold to the inside and burnish.

10. Align the completed accordion pages with the folded edge of the cover at left.

11. Wrap the remaining cover around the pages. Flip over, mark, and score the cover at the edge of the pages. Remove the pages.

12. Fold over the remaining flap at the score line.

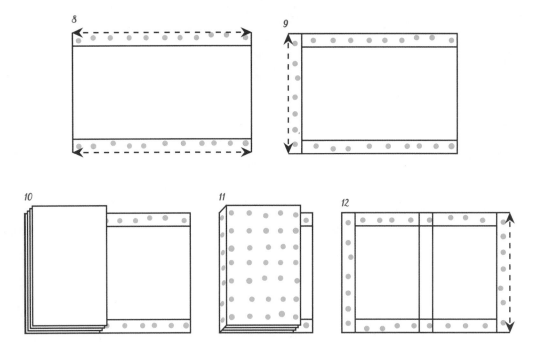

13. Trim all four corners of the flaps to a 45° angle.

14. Place the reinforcement paper within the cover folds. Trim the reinforcement paper to fit, if necessary.

15. With the ½" flap facing the fore edge of the front cover, place the pages back within the cover. Apply a thin layer of paste to the flap inside the front cover and adhere it to the front flap of the accordion.

16. Repeat, adhering the flap inside the back cover to the back page of the accordion. Press.

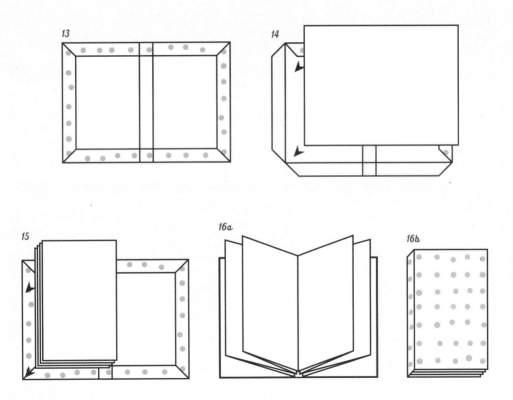

HARDCOVER INSTRUCTIONS

Finished Size

5 ⅞" × 9" × ½"

Tools

Metal ruler

Craft knife

Cutting mat or protective cutting surface

Pencil

Bone folder

Bulldog clip

Waxed paper

Paste or glue

Small and medium paste brushes

Book press or heavy stack of books

Materials

Drawing paper (medium weight): 10 pieces, each 12" × 9"

Book board: 2 pieces, each 5 ¾" × 9"

Book cloth: 1 piece, 14 ¼" × 11"

Instructions

1. Trim your papers to size with a metal ruler and craft knife.

2. Use a ruler and bone folder to score along the length of each inside page ½" from the left edge.

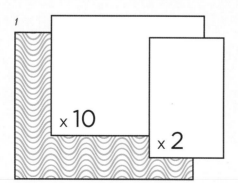

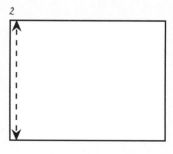

3. Fold each ½" flap to the back of the page. Burnish.

4. With the flap folded down, fold the remaining page in half, right to left. Burnish. Repeat, folding all inside pages in half.

5. Stack the folded pages with the folded flaps facing the same direction. Clip with a bulldog clip at the opposite side, away from the flaps. Place a small piece of scrap paper between the clip and the pages to prevent the clip from damaging the pages.

6. Lay the stack of pages with the top flap facing up. Starting at the bottom of the stack, tuck a small piece of waxed paper under a flap and apply paste to the flap. Adhere it to the next page. Repeat until all pages are connected. Press until dry.

7. Lay the piece of book cloth face down. Draw a line 1" from each edge to form a box in the center.

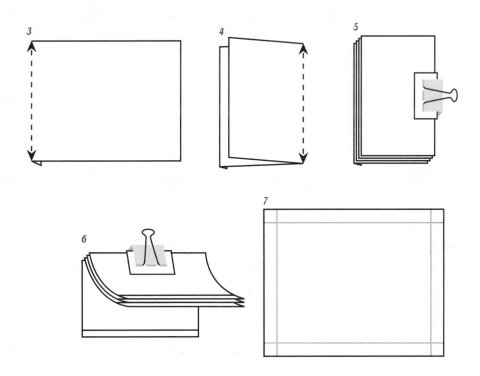

8. Trim all of the corners from the book cloth, leaving ¼" beyond each corner of the penciled-in box.

9. Apply a thin layer of paste to the back side of the book cloth. Align one piece of book board to the left of the box. Align the other piece of book board to the right of the box. There will be a gap between the two pieces. Flip the cover over onto a piece of waxed paper to smooth and remove air bubbles.

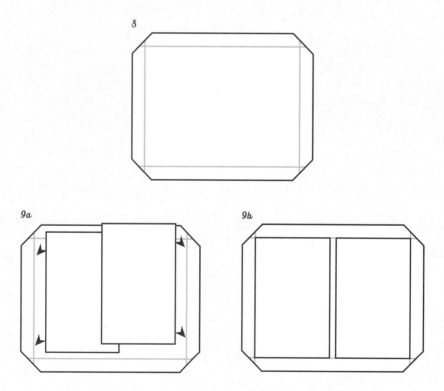

10. Flip again. Fold over the edges, long sides first and short sides last. Smooth. Press.

11. With the ½" flap facing the fore edge of the front cover, place the pages within the cover. Apply a thin layer of paste to the flap of the accordion and adhere it to the inside of the front cover.

12. Apply a thin layer of paste, ½" wide, to the back edge of the accordion and adhere it to the inside of the back cover. Press.

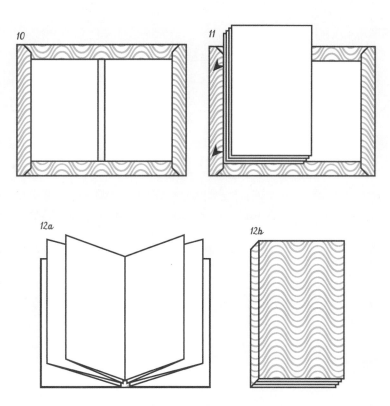

2

Outdoor Play

Take along a book to the big game, on your next bike ride, or to the pool. Unique materials make these projects great tagalongs for your favorite outdoor activities.

Treasure Hunt Collection Bag and Notebook

This is a great book to accompany a kids' scavenger hunt or treasure hunt. Both a bag and a book at the same time, this project allows each child to collect items and take notes too.

Finished Size

Varies

Tools

Metal ruler

Craft knife

Cutting mat or protective cutting surface

Pencil

Awl

Bone folder

Tapestry or binder's needle

Scissors

¼" hole punch

Materials

Small paper bag (choose a bag with a bottom that is about ⅓ the height of the bag)

Notebook paper: 5 pages, each equal to the bottom of the paper bag in height and double the bottom of the paper bag in width

Hole punch template: Equal to the size of the notebook paper

Small scrap of cardboard

Thread: 3 × the width of the bag

Hole reinforcement label

Ribbon or string: 4 × the height of the bag

Instructions

1. Measure the bottom panel of the paper bag. Use this measurement to determine the size of the pages. The height of each page will be equal to the longer measurement of the bottom panel. The width of each page will be double the shorter measurement of the bottom panel.

2. Trim your papers to size with a metal ruler and craft knife.

3. Fold each paper in half left to right. Also fold the template paper in half. Burnish.

4. Open the template paper and use the pencil to mark three holes along the inside of the fold. Make one mark directly in the center. Make a second mark centered between the center mark and the top edge of the template. Make a third mark centered between the center mark and the bottom edge of the template.

5. Nest all of the pages together. Place the template at the center of the pages. Punch holes at the marks through all layers. Remove the template paper.

6. Lay the paper bag flat with the bottom facing up, to your right. The opening of the bag will be to your left. Fold over the bottom end from right to left, creating a fold in the body of the bag directly next to the edge of the bottom panel. Burnish.

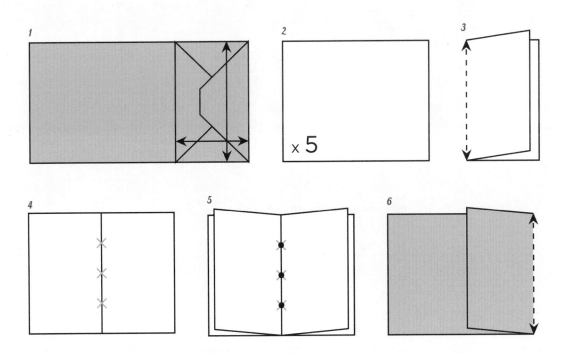

7. Fold the opening end from left to right in the same way, creating a fold in the body of the bag directly next to the folded-over bottom panel. Burnish. If the open end of the bag extends beyond the folded portion, trim the opening to line up with the fold.

8. Open up the folded bag so that it lies flat again and place a small piece of cardboard inside. Lay the center of the hole punch template along the right fold. The template will be next to the bottom of the bag. Punch through a single layer of the bag and into the cardboard at the marks on the template. Do not punch through both layers of the bag. Remove the template and cardboard.

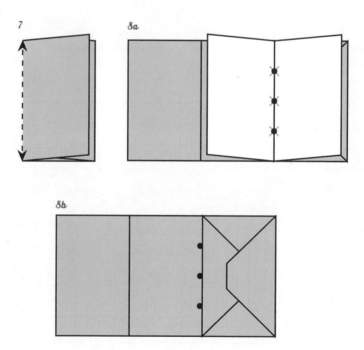

9. Align the punched pages with the punched holes in the bag. Sew the pages to the bag following the instructions for the ledger binding on pages 192–93. You will sew through the pages and one layer of the bag, to the inside of the bag. Open up the bag for easier sewing.

10. Once the pages are sewn in, fold the book so that the open end of the bag is to the right. Make a mark at the center of the front cover, ½" from the opening.

11. Use a ¼" hole punch to punch a hole at the mark. Place a hole reinforcement label at the back side of the hole.

12. Loop a ribbon or string through the hole to serve as a closure.

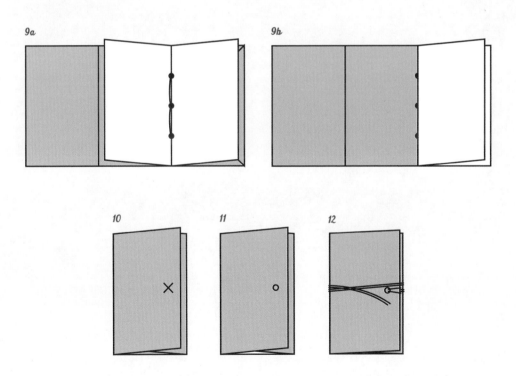

Little League Score Book

Keep track of your favorite baseball team all season long. With baseball card covers, you can pay homage to your favorite players too.

Finished Size

2 ¾" × 3 ½"

Tools

Metal ruler

Craft knife

Cutting mat or protective cutting surface

Bone folder

Pencil

Waxed paper

Paste, glue, or glue stick

Small paste brush (if using paste or glue)

Book press or heavy stack of books

Awl

Tapestry or binder's needle

Scissors

Materials

Card stock for spine: 1 piece, 2" × 3 ½"

Baseball cards: 2 cards, each 2 ½" × 3 ½"

Text weight paper: 10 pages, each 5" × 3 ½"

Template paper: Cut to inside page size, 5" × 3 ½"

String or thread: 10"

Instructions

1. Trim your papers to size with a metal ruler and craft knife.

2. Use a ruler and bone folder to score a line lengthwise down the center of the card stock. Draw two lines at either side of the score line, each ¼" from the score line.

3. Apply a thin layer of paste to the card stock, to the right side of the right line. Attach the left side of the front cover to the right side of the card stock, overlapping ¾". Apply a thin layer of paste to the card stock, to the left side of the left line. Attach the right side of the back cover to the left side of the card stock, overlapping ¾". There will be a ½" gap between the front and back cover. Press.

4. Fold each paper in half left to right, including the template paper. Burnish.

5. Open the template paper and use the pencil to mark three holes along the inside fold. Mark one hole directly in the center. Mark each of the other two holes halfway between the center hole and the edge of the page.

6. Nest the template within the pages and cover, centering the pages directly within the cover. Lay the book down on the cutting mat, cover facing down. Punch holes at the marks through all layers.

7. Sew the spine following the instructions for the ledger binding on pages 192–93. If necessary, press the completed book to flatten the spine.

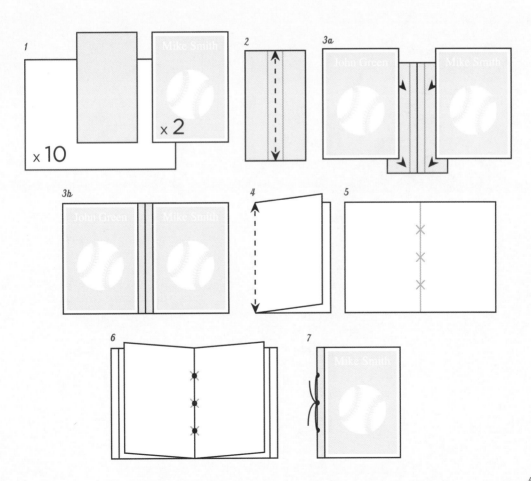

Waterproof Book

Whether you're beach-bound or pool-bound, this book is the perfect companion. Use a permanent pen or marker on these Tyvek pages and you have a waterproof writing solution.

Finished Size

6 ½" × 5"

Tools

Metal ruler

Craft knife

Cutting mat or protective cutting surface

Bone folder

Pencil

Awl or small hole punch

Tape

Bulldog clip

Tapestry or binder's needle

Scissors

Materials

Tyvek envelopes: about 3 envelopes, each 15" × 11 ½", cut into 12 pages, each
    13" × 5"

Template paper: 6 ½" × 5"

Waxed linen thread: 35"

Instructions

1. Trim your papers to size with a metal ruler and craft knife.

2. Fold each page in half right to left with the printed side facing in.
   Burnish. In traditional Japanese style, the folded edges will serve as the
   fore edges and the open edges will be bound into the spine.

3. Cut a piece of scrap paper to size to serve as a hole punch template.
   Mark a line ⅜" from the spine edge. Mark four holes along this line,
   one ⅝" from the top, another ⅝" from the bottom, and the third and
   fourth evenly distributed between the first two holes.

4. Working one page at a time, align the template along the spine, and
   punch holes at the marks with a small hole punch. The holes will be
   along the open edges of each page, opposite the folded edges. Tyvek is
   slick, so you may need to use removable tape to hold one page down at
   a time to the cutting mat as you punch.

5. Carefully line up the pages and clip with a bulldog clip at the fore edge. Place a small piece of scrap paper between the clip and the pages to prevent the clip from damaging the pages.

6. Stitch the spine following the instructions for the improvised Japanese four-hole binding on pages 180–85. Gently tighten the stitches as you go.

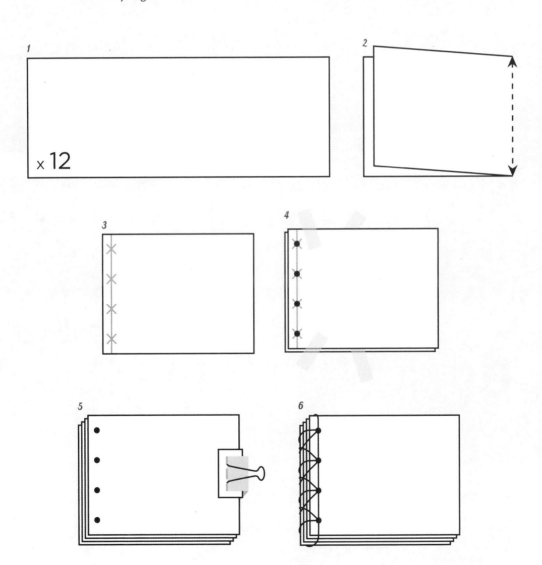

Bicycle Book

Repurposed bicycle tubes make great covers for this flexible, yet sturdy, little book. Toss it into your bike bag before your next ride and you will have a place to jot down notes on the go.

Finished Size

4" × 2 ½" × ⅜"

Tools

Metal ruler

Craft knife

Cutting mat or protective cutting surface

Scissors

Bone folder

Pencil

Bulldog clip

Awl

Small hole punch

Tapestry or binder's needle

Materials

Bicycle tube: 4 pieces, each 4" × 2 ½"

Double-sided adhesive sheet: 2 pieces, each 4" × 2 ½"

Text weight paper: 20–30 pages, each 4" × 2 ½"

Template paper: 4" × 2 ½"

Waxed linen thread: 40"

Instructions

1. Trim your papers and adhesive sheet to size with a metal ruler and craft knife.

2. Wash the bicycle tube with soap and water, rinse, and dry. Use a pair of scissors to cut across the tube and remove the valve area. Cut the tube open along a straight line so that you have one flat piece of rubber. Wash the rubber piece again. Dry thoroughly. Use a metal ruler and craft knife to cut the rubber into four 4" × 2 ½" pieces.

3. Apply one side of a double-sided adhesive sheet to the inside of one rubber piece. Smooth.

4. Attach another rubber piece to the adhesive sheet. Smooth. Your cover will be double-thickness. Repeat with the other cover.

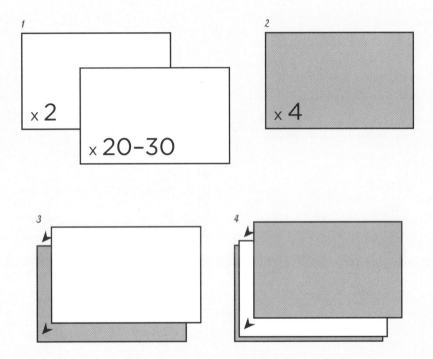

5. Create a hole punch template. Mark two lines, one ⅜" from the spine edge, and another ³⁄₁₆" from the spine edge. Mark four holes along the inner line, one ½" from the top, another ½" from the bottom, and the third and fourth evenly distributed between the first two holes. Mark five holes along the outer line, each one evenly distributed between the hole marks on the first line. The top and bottom holes will be between the hole marks on the first line and the edge of the template.

6. Carefully line up the inside pages and clip with a bulldog clip at the fore edge. Place a small piece of scrap paper between the clip and the pages to prevent the clip from damaging the pages.

5

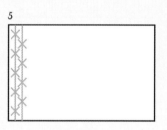

6

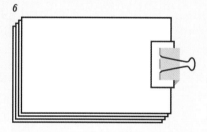

7. Align the template along the spine and punch holes in the pages at the marks.

8. Working one cover at a time, align the template along the spine and punch holes at the marks with a small hole punch.

9. Place the punched pages within the covers and stitch the spine following the instructions for the hemp-leaf binding on pages 164–71.

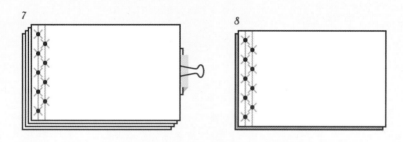

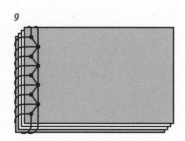

Texture Collector

This is the perfect spot to collect the many interesting textures that surround you. Flexible hinges allow each cover to open up completely so that you can place the transparent pages on any surface. Store a piece of graphite or charcoal in the capsule at the spine and use it to make rubbings anywhere.

Finished Size

12 ⅝" × 4 ½" × ½"

Tools

Metal ruler

Craft knife

Cutting mat or protective cutting surface

Pencil

Paste or glue

Small and medium paste brushes

Waxed paper

Book press or heavy stack of books

Bone folder

Bulldog clip

⅛" hole punch or Japanese screw punch

⅛" hollow punch or Japanese screw punch

Hammer (if using hollow punch)

Rubber bands

Needle with a large eye (to accommodate the elastic cord)

Needle nose pliers

Scissors

Materials

Tracing paper: 25 pieces, each 12" × 4 ½"

Newsprint: 25 pieces, each 12" × 4 ½"

Template paper: 12" × 4 ½"

Book board: 4 pieces, 2 pieces cut to ¾" × 4 ½" and 2 pieces cut to 10 ⅞" × 4 ½"

Text weight paper for hinges: 2 pieces, each 2" × 4 ½"

Decorative cover paper: 2 pieces, each 11 ⅞" × 6 ½"

Book cloth: 2 pieces, each 2 ½" × 6 ½"

Endpaper for inside of covers: 2 pieces, each 12" × 4 ½"

Elastic cord: 36"

Plastic tube with cap: 1 piece, about ½" × 4 ½" (you may need to cut a longer tube down to size)

Stick of charcoal or soft graphite: 1 piece, fits in plastic tube

Instructions

1. Trim your papers to size with a metal ruler and craft knife.

2. Draw two vertical lines in the center of each piece of hinge paper, leaving a ½" gap between the lines. The ½" gap will serve as a hinge in the cover.

3. Apply a thin layer of paste to the front of a piece of hinge paper. Line up a ¾" piece of book board along the left line of the hinge. Line up a 10 ⅞" piece of book board along the right line of the hinge. Flip the cover over and smooth. Press until dry. Repeat with the second cover. The finished size of each cover will be 12 ⅛" × 4 ½".

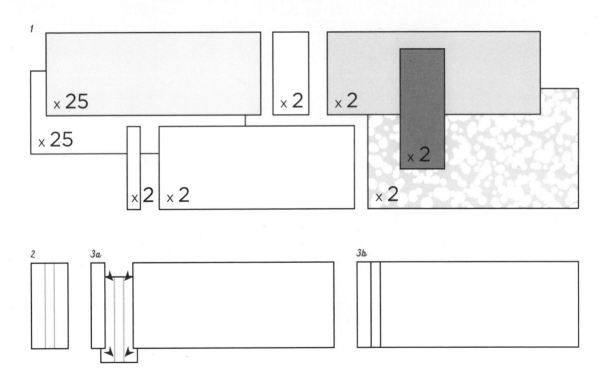

4. Draw a vertical line ¾" from the left edge of a cover paper.

5. Apply a thin layer of paste, ¾" wide, to the back edge of the book cloth. Attach the right side of the book cloth to the left side of the decorative cover paper, overlapping ¾". Press. Repeat with the other piece of book cloth and cover paper.

6. Lay out the completed cover papers face down. Draw a line 1" in from the top, bottom, and fore edge of each paper. Draw a line ½" in from the spine edge of each paper. The book cloth portion of each cover paper will be at the spine edge.

7. Trim all of the corners from the cover papers, leaving ¼" beyond each corner of the penciled-in boxes.

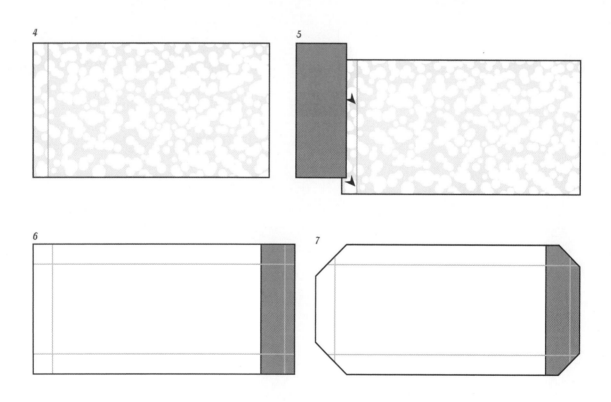

8. Apply a thin layer of paste to the back side of one cover paper. With the hinge facing the book cloth portion of the cover paper, place a hinged cover face down inside of the penciled-in box. Flip the hinged cover over onto a piece of waxed paper and smooth to remove air bubbles. Use the bone folder to carefully nudge the book cloth down into the hinge.

9. Flip again. Fold over the edges, long sides first and short sides last. Smooth.

10. Apply paste to a cover endpaper. Center the paper within the back side of the cover. Smooth. Press.

11. Repeat steps 7 through 10 with the other cover.

12. Cut a piece of scrap paper to size to serve as a hole punch template. Mark two lines, one ⅜" from the spine edge and another ³/₁₆" from the spine edge. Mark four holes along the inner line, one ⅝" from the top, another ⅝" from the bottom, and the third and fourth evenly distributed between the first two holes. Mark two holes along the outer line, one ⁵/₁₆" from the top, and the second ⁵/₁₆" from the bottom.

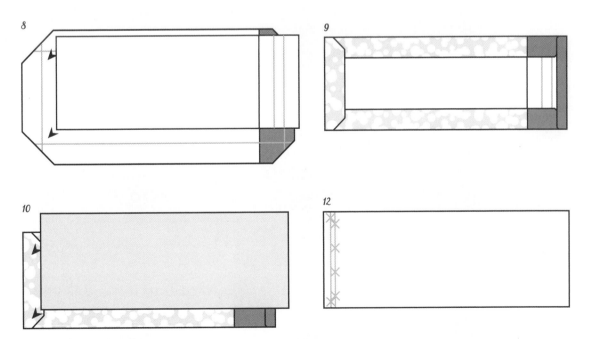

13. Carefully line up the tracing paper and newsprint pages, alternating between the two paper types: tracing paper, newsprint, tracing paper, newsprint, etc. Clip with a bulldog clip along the fore edge. Place a small scrap of paper between the clip and the pages to prevent the clip from damaging the pages.

14. Use the template to punch holes in the stack of pages along the spine. Use a ⅛" hole punch. You will need holes large enough to accommodate the thickness of your cord.

15. Working one cover at a time, align the template along the spine and punch holes at the marks with a ⅛" hollow punch.

16. Align the pages within the covers and secure with rubber bands. Align the plastic tube at the spine and secure with rubber bands.

13
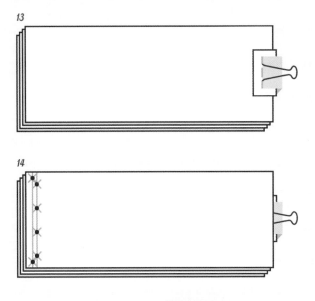

14

15

16
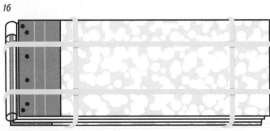

17. Stitch the spine following the instructions for the noble binding on pages 158–63. Here are a few tips specifically for this project:

   - To thread the needle, place a small piece of tape at the end of the elastic cord and flatten. Remove the tape before sewing.
   - Begin and end stitching at the inside, right between the back cover and the back page.
   - Stitch very loosely and tighten the stitches after you finish inside the back cover.
   - You may need to use a pair of needle nose pliers to pull the needle through the holes. Be very careful; stitching with elastic thread is tricky.
   - Stitch around the plastic tube with the two center stitches that wrap the spine. Remove the rubber bands from the tube as you stitch it into place.

18. Store a stick of charcoal or soft graphite in the plastic tube. Create rubbings of found textures on the tracing paper pages.

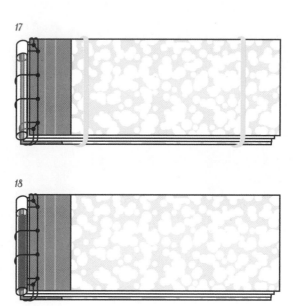

3

Nature Excursions

Enjoy the great outdoors with projects that allow you to collect leaves and flowers, discover the night sky, record the biggest catch, and jot down your own observations about it all.

Observation Journal

Jot down outdoor observations and more in this pocket-sized journal. Pages can alternate between blank and ruled so that there is plenty of room for both notes and sketches.

CHANNEL ISLANDS National Park

took a boat to Santa Cruz Island, from Ventura.

are 5 Islands that are part of the Channel Islands.

from the dock to the Scorpion Ranch campground
all our gear.

interesting animals:

- The island fox are the
scrub jay are some of the
Channel Islands are so
they don't live anywhere
in the world!

- We saw Bay
Sea Lion in the

Seaside
daisy

Finished Size

3 ½" × 5 ½"

Tools

Metal ruler

Craft knife

Cutting mat or protective cutting surface

Bone folder

Paste, glue, or glue stick

Small paste brush (if using paste or glue)

Waxed paper

Book press or heavy stack of books

Materials

Chip board or thick card stock: 2 pieces, cut to 3 ½" × 5 ½"

Text weight paper: 10 pieces, cut to 6 ¾" × 5 ⅜"

Adhesive label: 1 label, 2 ½" × 1"

Instructions

1. Trim your papers to size with a metal ruler and craft knife. If you like, use a corner rounder to round the corners of the pages and the fore edges of each cover.

2. Fold each paper in half left to right. Burnish.

3. Apply glue to the back of one folded paper in a ⅛" strip along the open edge. Adhere to the back of a second folded paper, aligning the open edges. Repeat until all 10 papers are attached to one another. Wrap in waxed paper and press until dry.

4. Apply glue to the entire back side of the first page of the accordion. Center the page within the back side of the front cover. Smooth.

5. Apply glue to the last page of the accordion. Center the page within the back side of the back cover. Smooth. Press flat until dry.

6. Attach the label at the center of the front cover.

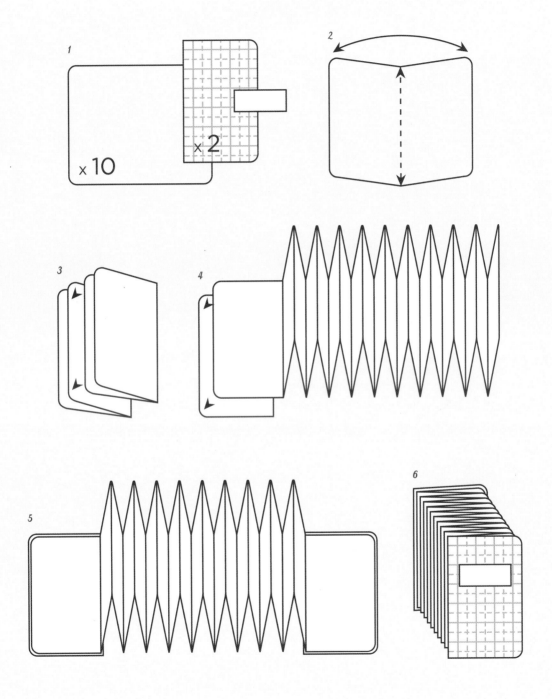

Leaf and Flower Press

Collect specimens on the go with this pretty accordion book. Place fresh leaves and flowers between the cardboard pages and wrap the straps closed to press.

Finished Size

5 ⅛" × 7 ⅛" × 2"

Tools

Metal ruler

Craft knife

Cutting mat or protective cutting surface

Pencil

Paste or glue

Small or medium paste brush (or both)

Waxed paper

Book press or heavy stack of books

Bone folder

Iron

Ironing board

Sewing machine or needle and thread

Tape

Hollow punch or Japanese screw punch

Hammer (if using hollow punch)

Materials

Cardboard: 10 pieces, each 5" × 7" × ⅛"

Text weight hinge paper: 9 pieces, each 1 ¼" × 7"

Book board: 2 pieces, each 5" × 7" × ⅛"

Book cloth or decorative cover paper: 2 pieces, each 7" × 9"

Blotting or drawing paper: 18 pieces, each 5" × 7"

Cotton straps: 2 pieces, each 1" × 22"

Iron-on hook and loop fasteners: 2 top pieces and 2 bottom pieces, each ¾" × 4"

Jean rivets: 2 pieces

Instructions

1. Trim your papers to size with a metal ruler and craft knife. Make sure that the grain of the cardboard and the hinges are parallel to the long side. Use a craft knife with a new blade to cut the cardboard.

2. Mark two vertical lines down the length of each hinge paper, ½" in from each side. There will be a ¼" gap between the two lines.

3. With the pencil-marked side facing up, apply glue to a hinge paper. Attach two pieces of cardboard to the hinge, aligning each to one of the vertical lines. There will be a ¼" gap between the two attached pieces of cardboard. Gently press until dry. Repeat with the other pieces of cardboard until you have five hinged pairs.

4. Turn over each hinged pair of cardboard pieces so that the hinge faces up. With the pencil-marked side facing up, apply glue to a new hinge paper. Attach two hinged pairs of cardboard pieces to the hinge paper, aligning each to one of the vertical lines. The first set of hinges and the newly adhered hinge will be on opposite sides of the cardboard. Repeat until all hinged pairs are attached into one long accordion. Leave the accordion open and gently press with books until dry. Do not press folded, or the pages may stick closed.

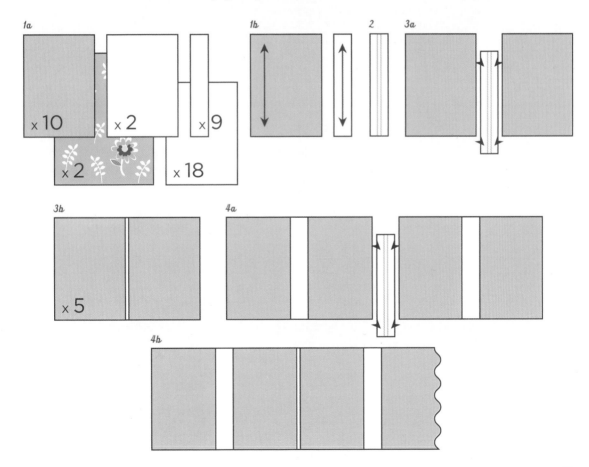

5. Lay the book cloth or decorative cover papers face down. Draw a line 1" in from each edge to form a 5" × 7" box in the center of the papers.

6. Trim all corners from the cover papers, leaving ¼" beyond each corner of the 5" × 7" box.

7. Determine which way the front and back cover papers are to face on the completed project. Use a pencil to mark the fore edge on the back side of each.

8. Apply a thin layer of glue to the back side of one cover paper. Place one of the book board pieces directly inside of the pencil-drawn box. Flip the glued board over onto a piece of waxed paper and smooth to remove air bubbles. Flip it again onto a clean surface. Fold over three of the edges: the unmarked spine side, the top, and the bottom. Do not fold over the marked fore edge. Smooth. Press until dry. Repeat with the other cover.

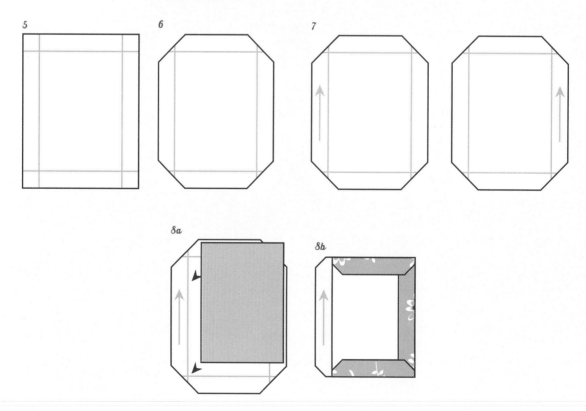

9. Lay a cotton strap flat and place a 4" piece of the soft loop side of a hook and loop fastener 2 ½" from the end of the strap. Center. Use a warm iron to attach, following the hook and loop fastener package instructions.

10. At the opposite end of the strap, fold the end under ½". Stitch to hem. You may need to apply a small amount of glue to prevent fraying.

11. Flip over the strap. Place a 4" piece of the remaining scratchy hook side of the hook and loop fastener ½" from the hemmed end. Center. Use a warm iron to attach, following the hook and loop fastener package instructions. The hook portion of the hook and loop fastener will be at the opposite end and on the opposite side of the strap from the loop portion.

12. Repeat steps 9–11 with the second strap.

13. Lay the straps on top of the front cover with ¾" of the unhemmed end extending past the spine edge. The soft loop side of the fastener will face up. Place one strap ¾" from the top and the other ¾" from the bottom of the cover. Use a gentle tape to hold the straps in place.

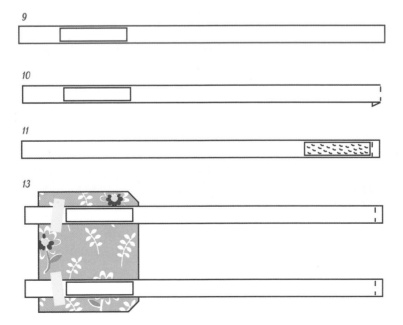

14. Use a pencil to mark the center of each strap ½" from the spine edge of the cover.

15. Punch or drill a ⅛" hole through the strap and cover at each mark. Apply a small amount of glue to each hole to prevent fraying.

16. Set a jean rivet at each hole following the jean rivet package instructions.

17. Wrap the ¾" extending strap edges around the spine to the inside of the cover. Glue into place. Allow to dry.

18. Fold the cardboard pages into an accordion. At each fold, the hinge paper will be at the outside of the fold. When the accordion is closed, there will be five hinges at the left. There will be four hinges, as well as the fore edge of the first and last pages, at the right. Note the orientation of the front and back pages. Open the accordion and lay flat.

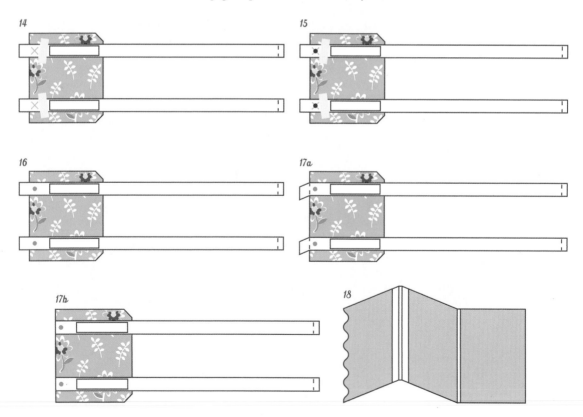

19. Apply glue to the inside of the back cover. Also apply glue to the inside of the cover paper extending at the fore edge. Attach the back cover to the back accordion panel. Wrap the extending cover paper around the fore edge of the back page.

20. Repeat step 19, attaching the front cover to the front page. Press until dry. Leave the accordion opened up flat to press. You may need to add extra weight to the front cover in order to press the straps flat at the spine.

21. Once it is dry, fold up the accordion. Place two blotting papers within each accordion fold. Place leaves and flowers between the blotting papers to press. Wrap the straps around the book and attach to keep closed.

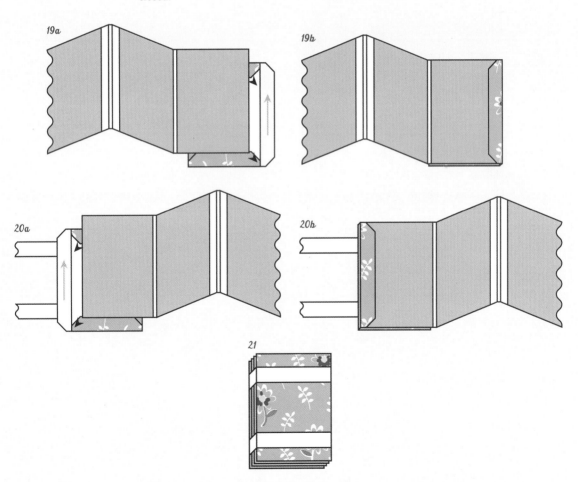

Gone Fishing Notebook

Accurately record who reels in the biggest catch of the day.
The spine of this book doubles as the tail of a fish, bound
with fishing line.

Finished Size

8" × 3" × ¼"

Tools

Metal ruler

Craft knife or scissors (or both)

Cutting mat or protective cutting surface

Pencil

Eraser

Bone folder

Waxed paper

Paste, glue, or glue stick

Small paste brush (if using paste or glue)

Book press or heavy stack of books

Bulldog clip

Awl

Tapestry or binder's needle

Scissors

Materials

Medium weight paper: 30 pages, each 8" × 3"

Decorative cover paper (a flexible Japanese-style paper is best): 2 pieces, each 9" × 4"

Endpaper for inside of covers (a flexible Japanese-style paper is best): 2 pieces, each 8" × 3"

Cover stock template paper: 8" × 3"

Fishing line: 35"

Instructions

1. Trim your papers to size with a metal ruler and craft knife.

2. Create an 8" × 3" fish-shaped template or use the template on page 85. Cut out the template.

3. Use a pencil to trace the template onto each page.

4. Cut out each page along the pencil line with scissors or a craft knife. Expect each page to vary just a bit in size once they are cut out.

5. Use a pencil to trace the template onto each endpaper.

6. Cut out each endpaper.

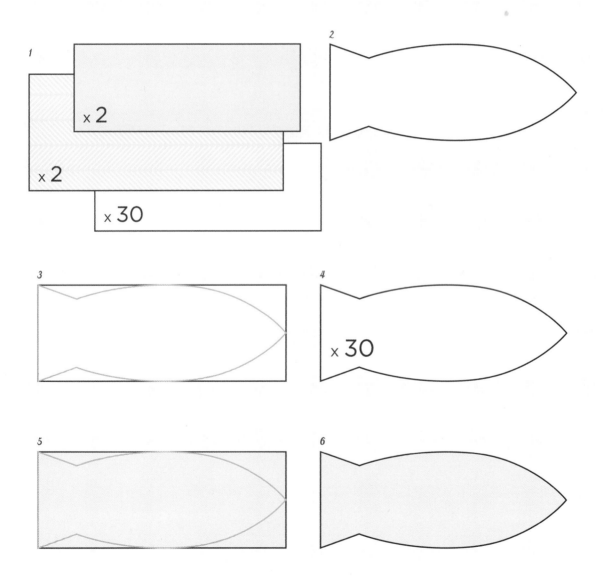

7. Use a pencil to trace the template onto the inside of the front cover paper. With the template still in place, score the cover paper along the outside of the template. Repeat, tracing and scoring the inside of the back cover paper.

8. Cut each cover into a fish shape, leaving a ½" border outside of the pencil line.

9. Use a craft knife or scissors to make several small cuts along the border of one cover, between the pencil line and the outside edge. Place a cut at every corner. Space the cuts about ½" apart along the rounded edges. Be careful to make the cuts outside of the pencil line. Repeat with the other cover.

10. Gently fold the border over at the score line toward the inside of the cover. Burnish. Repeat with the other cover.

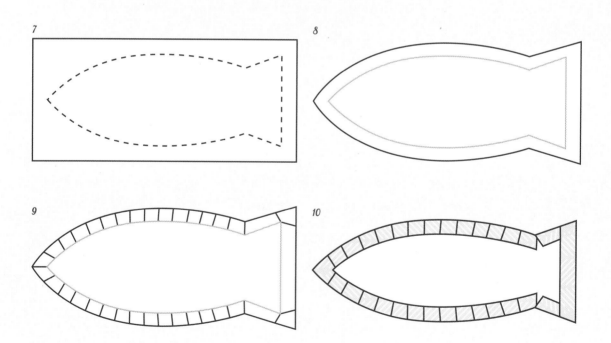

11. Place a small piece of waxed paper between the folded border and the inside of the cover. Use a glue stick or a small brush to apply a thin layer of glue to the border. Remove the wax paper while the glue is still wet. Place an endpaper onto the cover, adhering it to the border. Press until dry. Repeat with the other cover.

12. Mark the template to serve as a hole punch template. Draw a line 1 ¼" from the spine. Mark four holes along the line, evenly distributed between the top and bottom.

13. Carefully line up the inside pages within the covers and clip them together with a bulldog clip along the fore edge. Place a small scrap of paper between the clip and the covers to prevent the clip from damaging the covers.

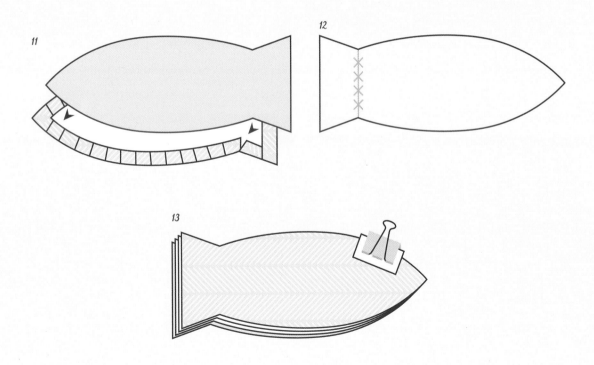

14. Use the template to punch holes in the stack of pages along the spine.

15. Stitch the spine following the instructions for the Japanese four-hole binding on pages 154–57.

16. Use a metal ruler and bone folder to gently score the front cover at the right side of the stitching.

14

15

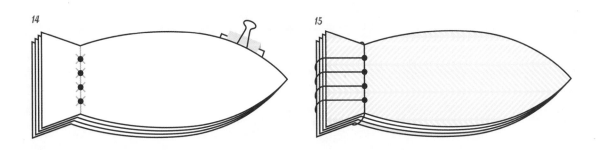

16

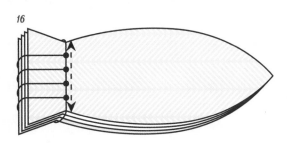

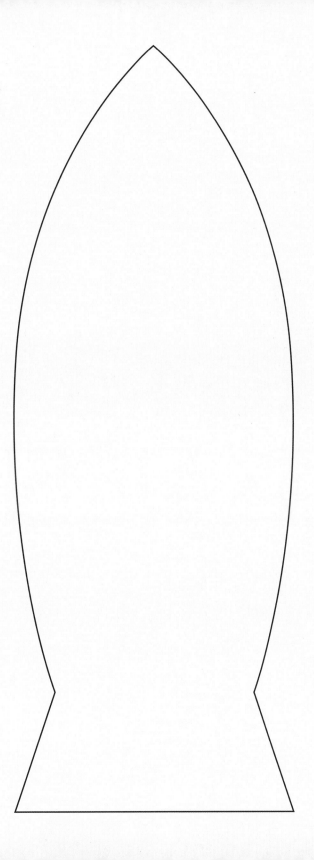

Star Gazing Log

Small holes punched through the front cover of this book reference the stars in the night sky. Bring it along on your next star gazing outing and note what you see.

Finished Size

8 ½" × 8 ½"

Tools

Metal ruler

Craft knife

Cutting mat or protective cutting surface

Bone folder

Tape

Hole punches, various sizes

Awl

Pencil

Bulldog clips

Tapestry or binder's needle

Scissors

Materials

Card stock (a dark color): 2 pieces, 11" × 8 ½"

Star map: 1 printout, 8 ½" × 11"

Text weight end sheet (bright white): 1 page, 8 ½" × 8 ½"

Text weight paper (ruled): 30–50 pages, each 8 ½" × 8 ½"

Waxed linen thread: 50"

Instructions

1. Trim your papers to size with a metal ruler and craft knife. Go online to find a star map and print it on an 8 ½" × 11" page, photocopy a star map from a book, or draw your own.

2. Lay the covers on a cutting mat horizontally. Use the bone folder and ruler to score the cover papers from top to bottom, 2 ½" from the right edge. This will create an 8 ½" cover panel and a 2 ½" flap.

3. Use removable tape to hold the front cover to the cutting mat. Place the star map over the 8 ½" × 8 ½" cover panel and tape it down as well.

4. Use various sizes of hole punches to punch out the stars, punching through both layers. Use an awl to punch the smallest stars. Leave a ½" strip at the spine unpunched for stitching.

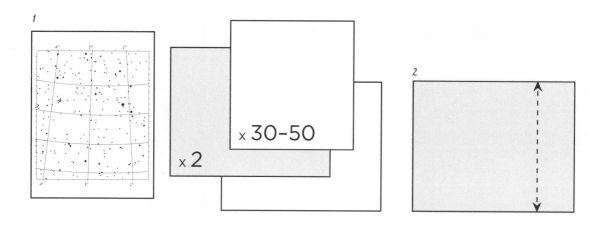

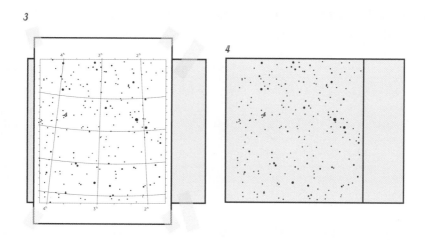

5. Fold the 2 ½" flap to the inside of each cover. Burnish.

6. Cut a piece of scrap paper to size to serve as a hole punch template. Mark two lines, one ⅜" from the spine edge and another ³⁄₁₆" from the spine edge. Mark four holes along the inner line, one ⅝" from the top, another ⅝" from the bottom, and the third and fourth evenly distributed between the first two holes. Mark eight holes along the outer line, each one ¼" to either side of the hole marks on the first line.

7. Place the end sheet at the front of the stack of pages. Carefully line up the inside pages and end sheet within the covers and clip them together with a bulldog clip along the fore edge. Place a small scrap of paper between the clip and the covers to prevent the clip from damaging the covers.

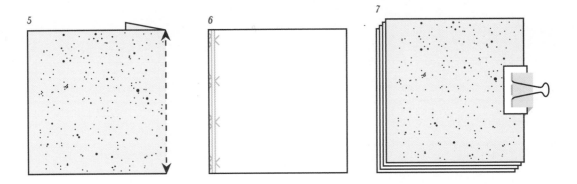

8. Use the template to punch holes in the stack of pages along the spine.

9. Stitch the spine following the instructions for the tortoise-shell binding on pages 172–79.

10. Use a metal ruler and bone folder to gently score the front cover at the right side of the stitching.

11. Tuck the end sheet into the front cover flap. If the end sheet is too long, trim it to fit.

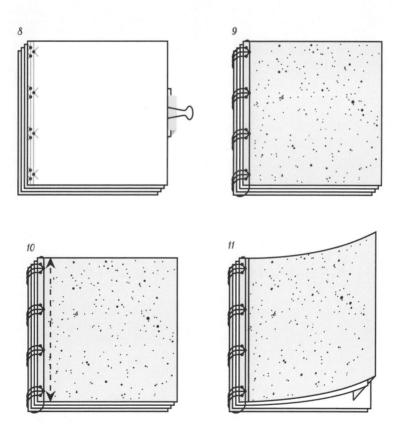

Camping Songbook

Print out your favorite camp songs and bind them into this fun book. The canvas cover rolls up and ties closed with a ribbon to protect the pages. Unroll and reference the music when you are ready to sing along.

Finished Size
8 ¾" × 14"

Tools
Pencil

Ruler

Bulldog clips

Awl

Cutting mat or protective cutting surface

Fabric scissors

Fabric pins

Iron

Ironing board

Sewing machine

Sharp sewing needle with a medium eye

Materials
Text weight paper: 10 pages, each 8 ½" × 11"

Template paper: 8 ½" × 11"

Canvas, denim, or twill fabric: Cut to 10" × 16"

Sewing thread to match fabric

Twill tape or ribbon: ⅜" wide × 26"

Waxed linen thread or heavy sewing thread: 40"

Instructions

1. Print your favorite camp songs onto 8 ½" × 11" text weight paper or choose to use blank pages and write the songs down later.

2. Use an extra 8 ½" × 11" page to serve as a hole punch template. Mark a line ⅜" from the spine edge. Mark four holes along this line, one ⅝" from the top, another ⅝" from the bottom, and the third and fourth evenly distributed between the first two holes.

3. Carefully line up the inside pages and clip them together with a bulldog clip along the fore edge. Place a small scrap of paper between the clip and the pages to prevent the clip from damaging the pages.

4. Use the template to punch holes in the stack of pages along the spine. If your music is printed in portrait mode, place the holes at the top. If your music is printed in landscape mode, place the holes at the left.

5. Cut the fabric piece and ribbon to size.

6. Along the length of the fabric, fold the edges over ¼" and press with a hot iron. Fold the edges over ¼" a second time and press with a hot iron. Pin if needed.

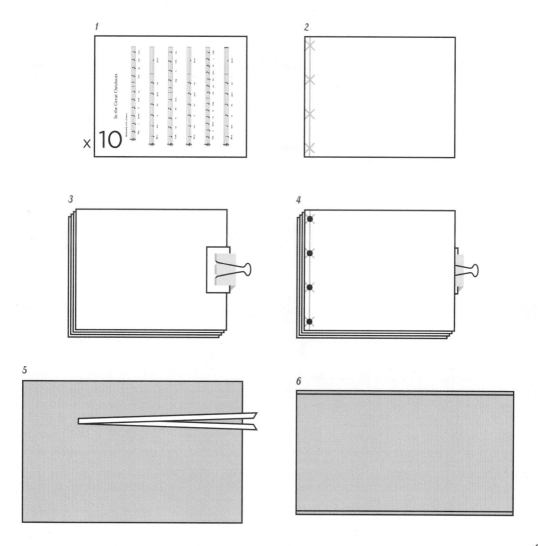

7. Using a sewing machine, stitch along the length of the folds, ⅛" in from the edge. Each folded and stitched edge is a hem.

8. Along one short end of the fabric, fold the edge over ¼" and press with a hot iron. Fold the edge over ¼" a second time and press with a hot iron. Pin if needed. Using a sewing machine, stitch along the length of the hem, ⅛" in from the edge.

9. Fold the twill tape or ribbon in half. Place the center fold of the twill tape at the center of the short hemmed edge of the fabric. Pin if needed. Stitch into place.

10. Along the unhemmed side of the fabric, fold the edge over ½" and press with a hot iron. Fold the edge over ½" a second time and press again with a hot iron.

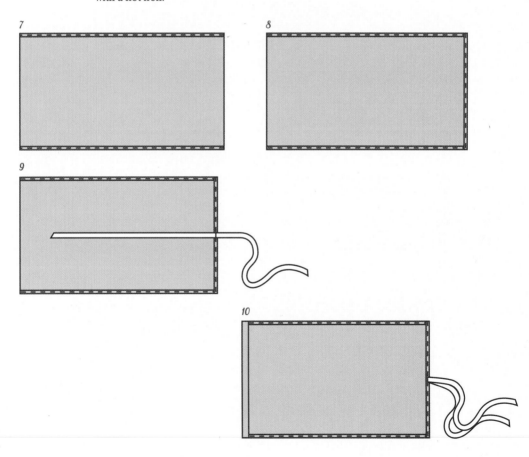

11. Slide the punched edge of the stack of pages underneath the ½" folded edge of the fabric, making sure to place the pages snugly against the inside of the fold. Clip the fabric and the pages together at the spine with several bulldog clips. You will remove the clips as you stitch.

12. Stitch the spine following the instructions for the Japanese four-hole binding on pages 154–57. Stitch directly through the fabric. Because you cannot see the binding holes from the outside, you may need to poke around for the holes until the end of your needle finds them. Be careful at the top and bottom, as the fabric may pucker.

13. To close the book, roll from the spine toward the fore edge and tie with the twill tape.

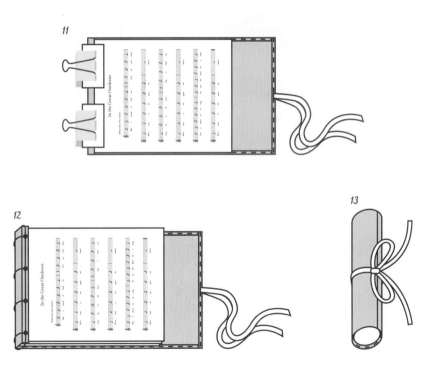

4

Road Trips

Hit the road with the perfect travel companion. These book projects encourage you to list fun places to visit, send notes from the road, keep track of your travel photos, and make use of your travel memorabilia.

Tiny Tickets Memorabilia Book

Save your boarding passes and tickets to use as covers for this tiny notebook. With pages cut to the same size as the cover and a simple binding, your memorabilia takes on a new life.

Leeum Day-Pass

ONE

茶室廳拝観物

Finished Size

Varies (will depend on the size of your boarding pass or ticket)

Tools

Metal ruler

Craft knife

Cutting mat or protective cutting surface

Pencil

Bulldog clip

⅛" hole punch or Japanese screw punch

Scissors

Materials

Boarding pass or ticket: 1 piece

Text weight paper: 20 pages, cut to cover size

Card stock: 1 piece, cut to cover size

Template paper: Cut to cover size

Cotton braiding cord: 6"

Instructions

1. Measure the dimensions of your boarding pass or ticket.

2. Trim your papers to the size of your boarding pass or ticket with a metal ruler and craft knife.

3. Cut a piece of scrap paper to the cover size to serve as a hole punch template. Mark a line ¼" from the spine edge. Mark two holes along this line, evenly distributed between the edges of the page.

4. Arrange your papers in order: card stock on bottom, pages in the middle, and the ticket facing up on the top. Clip with a bulldog clip along the fore edge. Place a small scrap of paper between the clip and the pages to prevent the clip from damaging the pages.

5. Use the template to punch holes through the entire thickness at the spine. A ⅛" hole punch will accommodate the thickness of your cotton cord.

6. Stitch the spine following the instructions for the Yamato binding on pages 186–87. If your holes are large enough, you will not need to

stitch with a needle but can thread the cotton cord directly through the holes.

7. Use a metal ruler and bone folder to gently score the front cover at the right side of the stitching.

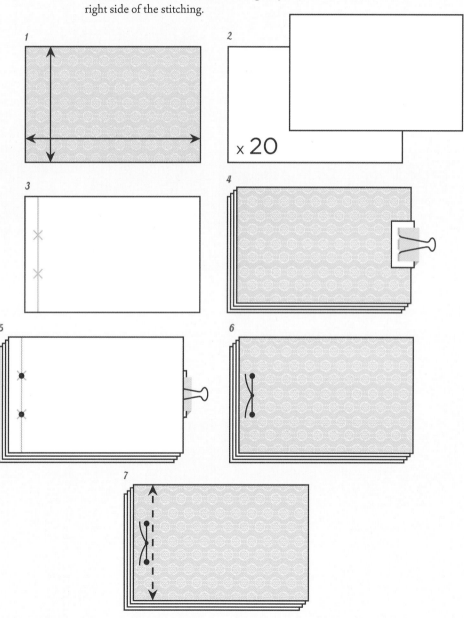

Photo Notes

This is a great way to reuse old processed film, which serves as the covers for this small book. Tie one or several to your camera during your next outing to take note of camera settings or anything else you'd like to remember.

Finished Size

3" × 1 ⅜"

Tools

Metal ruler

Craft knife

Cutting mat or protective cutting surface

Pencil

Bulldog clip

Awl

Small hole punch or 2mm Japanese screw punch

Scissors

Materials

Text weight paper: 30 pages, each 3" × 1 ⅜"

Hole punch template: 3" × 1 ⅜"

Processed film strip: 2 pieces, each 3" × 1 ⅜"

Waxed linen thread: 2 strands, each 15"

Instructions

1. Trim your papers and film strip to size with a metal ruler and craft knife. Make sure that the grain of each paper is parallel to the short side.

2. Create a hole punch template. Mark a line ¼" from the spine edge. Mark two holes along this line, evenly distributed between the top and bottom of the page.

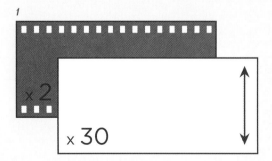

3. Carefully line up the pages and clip with a bulldog clip at the fore edge. Place a small piece of scrap paper between the clip and the pages to prevent the clip from damaging the pages.

4. Line up the template at the spine and punch holes in the stack of pages at the marks.

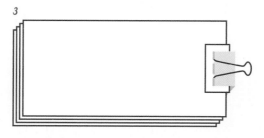

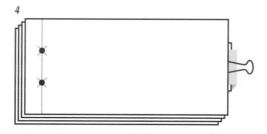

5. Line up the template with the front cover and punch holes at the marks with a hole punch or 2mm Japanese screw punch. Repeat with the back cover.

6. Remove the bulldog clip from the pages. Carefully align the pages between the covers and clip with a bulldog clip along the fore edge. Place a small scrap of paper between the clip and the covers to prevent the clip from damaging the covers.

5

6

7. Stitch the spine following the instructions for the account book binding on pages 188–91.

8. Use a metal ruler and bone folder to gently score the front cover at the right side of the stitching.

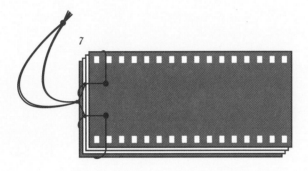

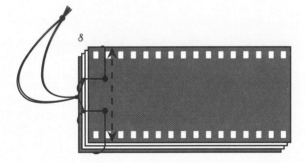

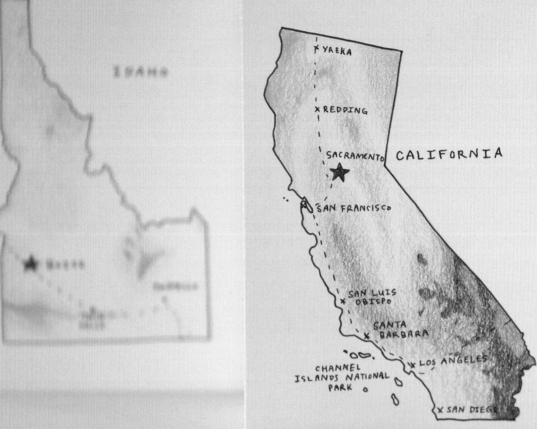

Notes from the Road
Postcard Book

This book is similar to a vintage postcard booklet, except you create the art. Bring a blank book along and fill out the pages as you go. Simply tear off a page at the perforation, address and add a stamp, and drop in a mailbox.

ARIZONA

Finished Size

4 ½" × 6" × ⅛"

Tools

Metal ruler

Craft knife

Cutting mat or protective cutting surface

Pencil

Bone folder

Rotary perforator

Paste, glue, glue stick, or double-sided tape

Small paste brush (if using paste or glue)

Waxed paper (if using paste or glue)

Book press or heavy stack of books (if using paste or glue)

Materials

Card stock cover: 1 piece, cut to 6" × 11"

Poster board pages (a thin poster board works best): 1 piece, cut to 6" × 24 ½"

Instructions

1. Trim your papers to size with a metal ruler and craft knife.

2. Starting at the left side, use the ruler and pencil to measure and mark the placement of the folds along the length of the card stock at these measurements: 4 ½" and 9".

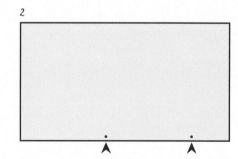

3. Use a ruler and bone folder to score the card stock at each of the fold marks. This will create two 6" × 4 ½" panels and one 2" flap. Fold the cover at the scored lines and burnish. Unfold.

4. Use a pencil to mark each corner of the cover flap. Mark 1 ½" away from the corner toward the fold and mark 1" away from the corner toward the center. Draw a straight line between the two marks at each corner. To mark the slit for the flap, make two pencil marks 1 ½" in from the left edge of the cover. Mark once ⅝" in from the top and again ⅝" in from the bottom. Draw a straight line between the two marks.

5. Use a metal ruler and craft knife to cut along the pencil marks. Check your measurements by tucking the flap into the slit.

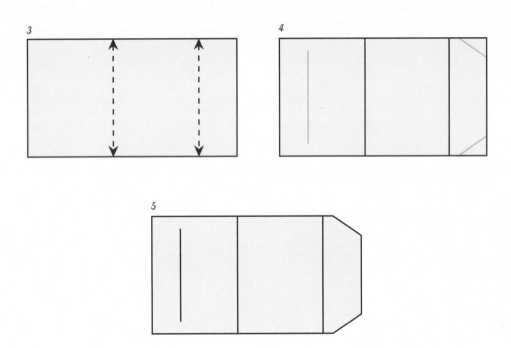

6. Use the ruler and pencil to measure and mark the accordion folds along the bottom of the poster board at these measurements: 4", 8", 12", 16", 20", 24".

7. Use a rotary perforator to perforate the poster board at each of the fold marks.

8. Fold the ½" flap to the back. Continue to fold the rest of the pages into an accordion.

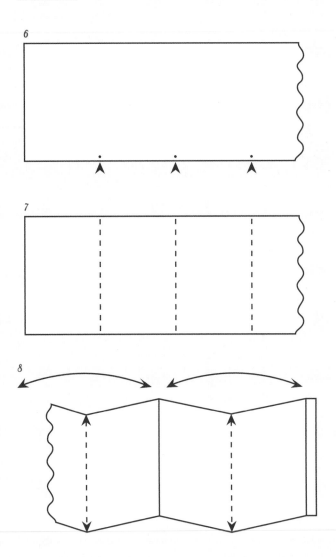

9. Apply a thin layer of glue or double-sided tape to the ½" flap. Center the folded pages within the cover, with the glued flap toward the cover flap. Adhere the flap to the inside of the cover. Press until dry.

10. To use, tear off a postcard along the perforation.

11. Tuck the flap in to close the book.

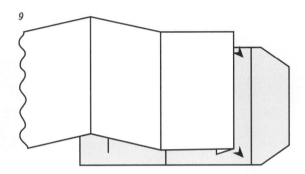

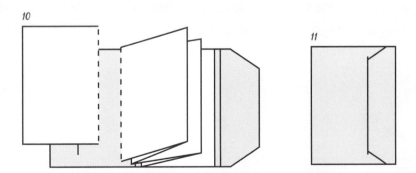

Fold-Out Map Booklet

Keep this little booklet in your pocket and you can find your way around just about anywhere. Choose a destination, print a map, and fold it up into a small accordion. A wraparound cover and button and string closure protect the map so that you can use it again and again.

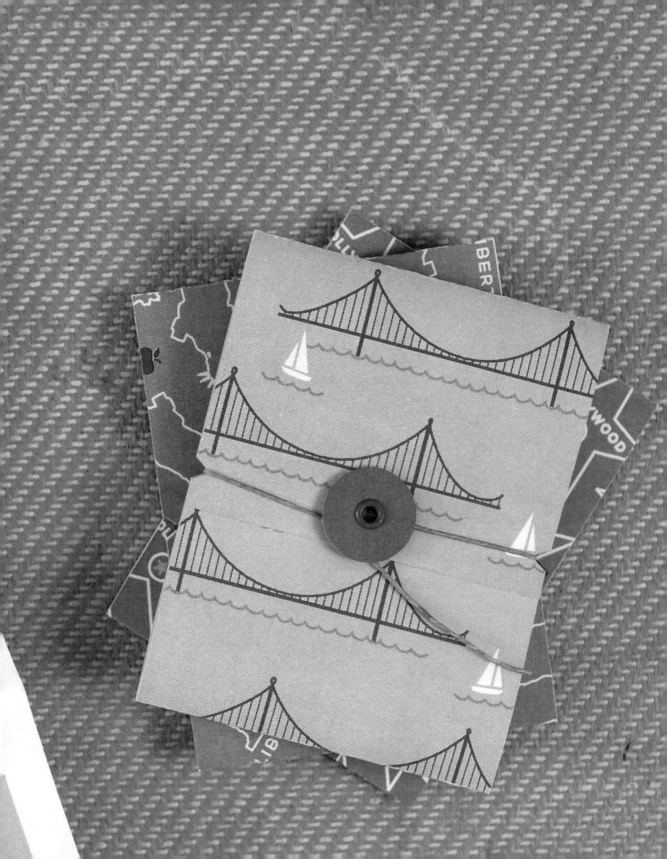

Finished Size

2 ½" × 3 ¼" × ⅛"

Tools

Metal ruler

Craft knife

Cutting mat or protective cutting surface

Pencil

Bone folder

⅛" hole punch

⅝" circle punch

Eyelet-setting tool

Scissors

Double-sided tape

Materials

Card stock cover: 1 piece, 2 ½" × 7 ⅛"

Card stock circle (a thick card stock is best): 1 circle, ⅝" in diameter

Eyelet: 1 eyelet, ⅛" in diameter

Linen thread or cotton cord: 10"

Text weight map printout: 1 page, 8 ½" × 11"

Template paper: 2 ½" × 7 ⅛"

Instructions

1. Trim your papers to size with a metal ruler and craft knife.

2. Starting at the top, use the ruler and pencil to measure and mark the placement of the folds along the length of the card stock at these measurements: 1 ⅞" and 5 ⅛".

3. Use a ruler and bone folder to score the card stock at each of the fold marks.

4. At the inside of the cover, mark a line ¼" from the top edge. Along the line, mark a ⅛" notch at each side. Mark a ⅛" hole along the line, directly at the center of the cover.

5. Use a craft knife to cut out the notches. Use a hole punch to make a ⅛" hole at the center mark.

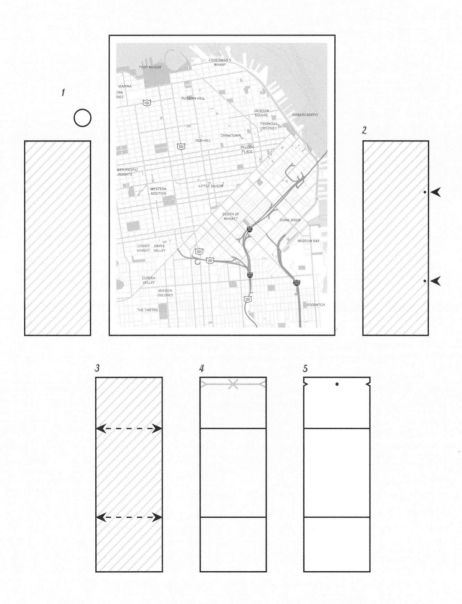

6. Fold up the bottom flap, then fold down the top flap. Burnish.

7. At the two notches in the top cover, cut down through all layers.

8. Punch a ⅝" circle out of thick card stock. Punch a ⅛" hole directly at the center of the circle. This will serve as the button.

9. Place a ⅛" eyelet through the center hole of the button.

10. At the back side of the button, tie one end of the thread around the eyelet shaft.

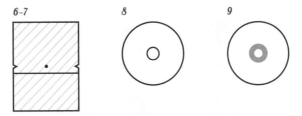

11. With the button and string attached, place the eyelet through the hole in the front of the cover and set it with an eyelet-setting tool.

12. To fold the map, lay it face down and fold it in half lengthwise. Burnish.

13. Fold each side over to touch the center fold, as you would an accordion fold. Burnish.

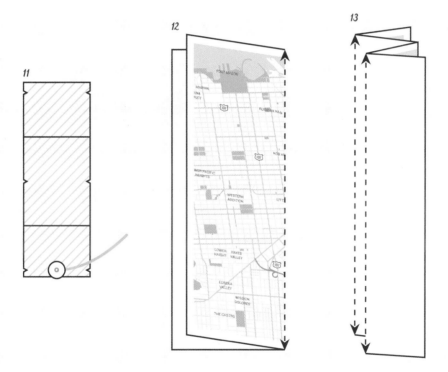

14. With the open edges of the map to the right, bring the bottom of the folded page up to meet the top. Burnish.

15. Fold the open edges down to meet the center fold. Burnish. The folded map will measure 2 ⅛" × 2 ¾".

16. Find the top left corner of the map. Apply double-sided tape to the back of this section.

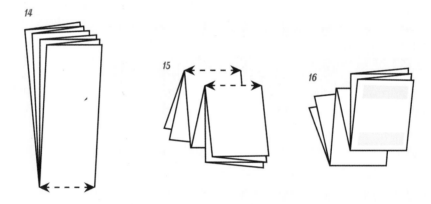

17. Center the folded map within the cover and attach. When the map unfolds, it will pull down and to the right of the cover.

18. Fold up the bottom flap, then fold down the top flap. Wrap the string around the cover at the notches and attach to the button to close.

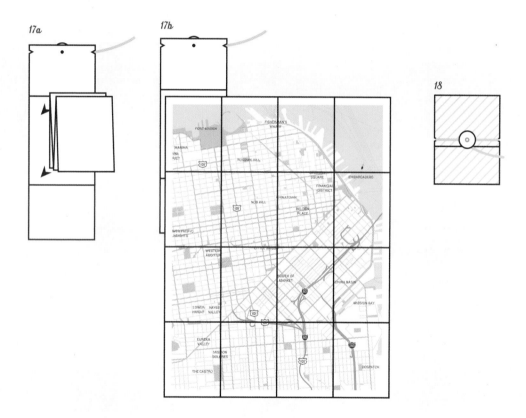

17a

17b

18

Things to Check Out Book

Library pockets form the pages of this unique book. Use each card to keep a list of places to go and things to do. You can even remove a library card and bring it with you to take notes on the go. Return the card to its pocket when done to keep a record of your outings.

Finished Size

4 ⅛" × 5 ½" × ½"

Tools

Metal ruler

Craft knife

Cutting mat or protective cutting surface

Pencil

Eraser

Waxed paper

Paste, glue, or glue stick

Small paste brush (if using paste or glue)

Book press or heavy stack of books

Bone folder

⅛" hole punch

⅝" circle punch

Eyelet-setting tool

Corner-rounding punch

Bulldog clip

Awl

Tapestry or binder's needle

Scissors

Materials

Pocket envelopes: 10, each 3 ½" × 4 ⅛"

Text weight hinge paper: 10 pieces, each 1" × 3 ⅝"

Card stock spine reinforcement (a thick card stock is best): 10 pieces, each ⅜" × 3 ⅝"

Card stock cover (a thick card stock is best): 4 ¾" × 12 ⅝" (grain short)

Card stock circles (a thick card stock is best): 2, each ⅝" in diameter

Eyelets: 2, each ⅛" in diameter

Cotton jewelry cord or unwaxed linen thread (a thin string is best): 8"

Hole punch template: ⅜" × 3 ⅝"

Waxed linen thread: 5"

Library cards: 10, each 3" × 5"

Instructions

1. Trim your papers to size with a metal ruler and craft knife. Collect the library pocket envelopes or use the template on page 135 to create your own.

2. Lay a pocket envelope face down on a flat surface and use a ruler and pencil to mark a line ½" in from the right edge. Repeat, marking the back side of all ten envelopes.

3. Lay a hinge paper on a flat surface and use a ruler and pencil to mark a line lengthwise down the center of the paper. Repeat, marking all ten hinges.

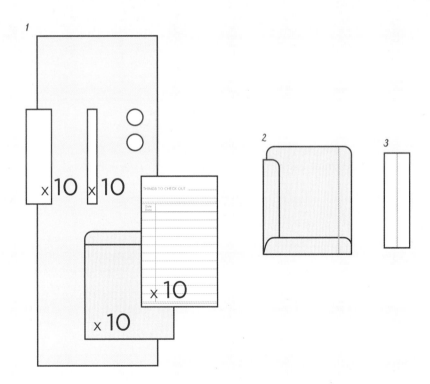

4. Lay a hinge paper on waxed paper and apply glue to one side of the pencil line. Attach the paper to the back side of a pocket envelope. The paper will line up with the pencil line marked on the envelope as well as with the bottom of the envelope. Press. Repeat with the other hinges and pocket envelopes.

5. Lay a pocket envelope face up with the attached hinge paper at the left side. Apply glue to a card stock spine reinforcement piece and attach it to the left side of the exposed hinge paper. Press. Repeat, attaching all reinforcement pieces to the pocket envelope hinges.

6. Mark the card stock cover along the length at 3", 8 ½", and 9" from the top. Score the cover at each of these marks.

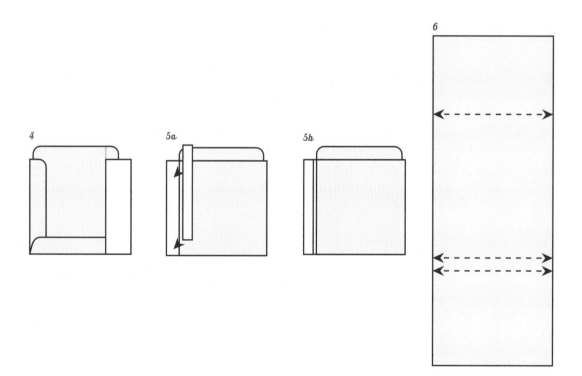

7. Use a pencil to mark a line ⅝" in from the right edge. Along this line, make a mark at 4 ⅞" and at 8 ½" from the top.

8. Use a metal ruler and craft knife to cut along the pencil line above and below the two marks. Cut from the marks toward the edge of the cover, removing the two excess pieces of card stock.

9. Score the remaining extension along the pencil line.

10. Your cover is now 4 ⅛" × 12 ⅝" plus the extension. Lay the cover on a flat surface with the extension to the right. At the center of the cover, mark a hole ¾" from the top edge and another 1 ¾" from the bottom edge.

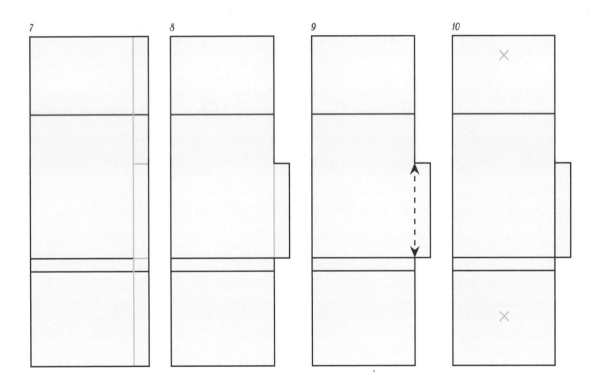

11. Use a hole punch to make a ⅛" hole at each of the two marks.

12. Punch two ⅝" circles out of thick card stock. Punch a ⅛" hole directly at the center of each circle. These will serve as the buttons.

13. Place a ⅛" eyelet through the center hole of one button.

14. At the back side of the button, tie one end of the cotton jewelry cord or unwaxed linen thread around the eyelet shaft.

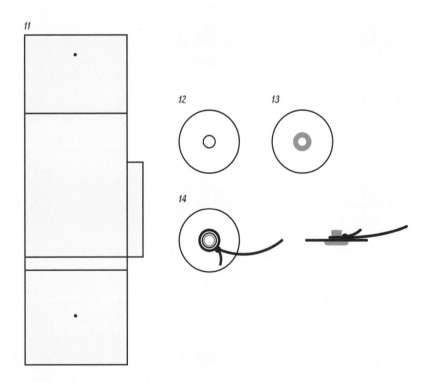

15. With the button and string attached, place the eyelet through the top hole in the cover and set it with an eyelet-setting tool.

16. Place the other ⅛" eyelet through the center hole of the remaining button. With the button attached, place the eyelet through the bottom hole in the cover and set it with an eyelet-setting tool.

17. Use a corner-rounding punch to round all four corners of the cover.

18. Carefully align the pocket envelopes with attached hinges and spine reinforcements and clip with a bulldog clip at the fore edge. Place a small piece of scrap paper between the clip and the pages to prevent the clip from damaging the pages.

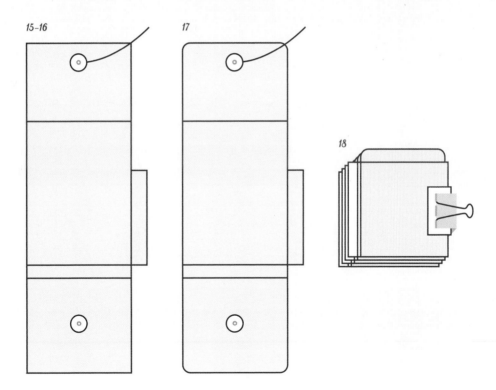

19. Place the clipped pages inside the cover, next to the extension.

20. Fold the extension around the spine and over the front of the pages. If needed, trim the extension so that it aligns with the spine reinforcements attached to the hinges. The final size of the front flap of the extension will be ⅜" × 3 ⅝".

21. Create a hole punch template. Mark a line ³⁄₁₆" from the spine edge. Mark two holes along this line, evenly distributed between the top and bottom of the template.

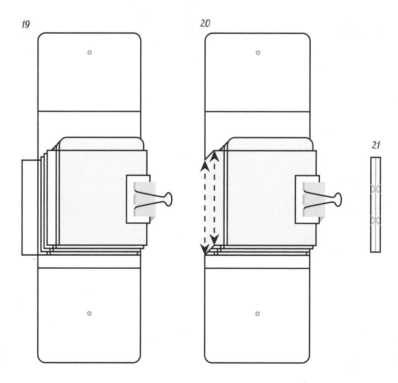

22. Open up the cover and align the hole punch template with the front of the extension on a cutting mat or protective surface. Punch through the front of the extension at the marks. You will not punch through the back of the cover.

23. Use the template to punch holes in the pages along the spine.

24. Realign the pages beneath the cover. Stitch the pages to the front extension of the cover following the instructions for the Yamato binding on pages 186–87.

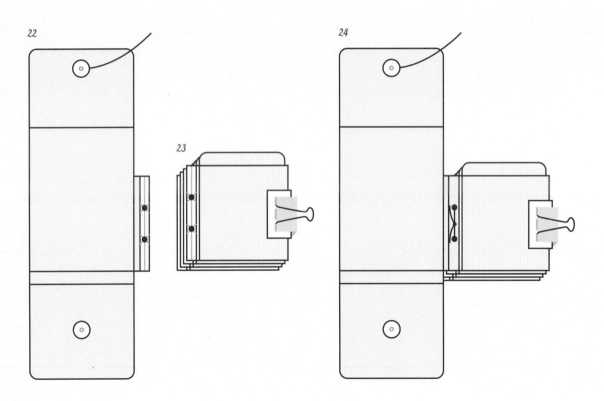

25. Fold the pages back over into the cover and remove the bulldog clip.

26. Place a library card within each library pocket.

27. Fold up the bottom flap of the cover, then fold over the top flap to enclose the pages. Wind the string between the buttons to close.

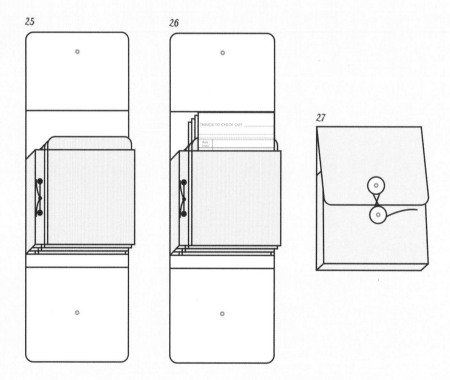

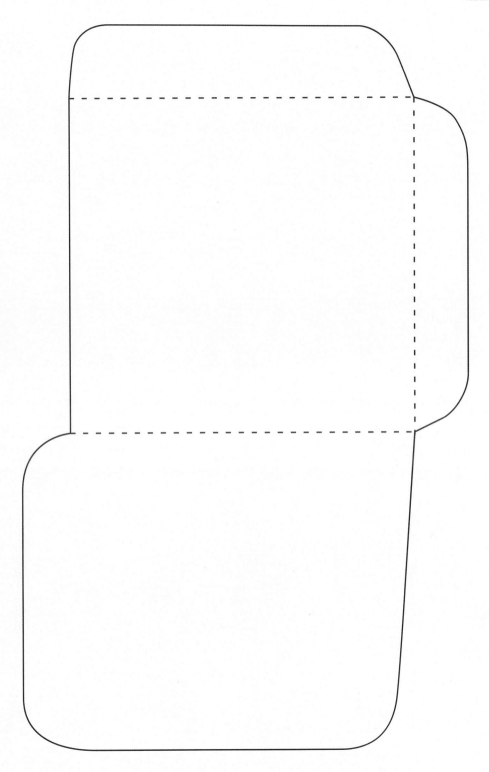

Bookbinding Tools and Materials

Many bookbinding tools and materials are used for a variety of other arts and crafts. This makes collecting them fairly easy. You may discover that you already have many of these supplies.

The basic ingredients for a book include paper and string. Tools for cutting, pasting, punching, and stitching turn these basic ingredients into a finished product.

TOOLS

Some of the projects in this book call for the use of tools other than those specific to bookbinding. The tools required for any given project in this book are listed below, but you do not need to collect them all. The most important bookbinding tools are starred (*). Most of these tools are available at arts and crafts supply stores.

*1.   *Bone folder:* One of the most versatile bookbinding tools, a bone folder is made to score, smooth, and burnish paper. Sharpen with sandpaper as needed.

2.   *Wood potter's rib:* This inexpensive tool is great for smoothing and burnishing paper.

*3.   *Pencil:* Use an erasable pencil to mark your projects. A sharp point results in more accurate marks.

*4.   *Eraser:* A vinyl or gum eraser will remove pencil marks from most projects.

*5.   *Tapestry needle and binder's needle:* Look for a needle with an eye large enough to accommodate your thread. A blunt tip helps to save your fingers while stitching.

6.   *Beeswax:* Apply wax to unwaxed thread for smoother stitching. Waxed thread is especially useful for stab bindings.

7.   *Rubber bands:* This basic office supply is useful for holding materials together when a bulldog clip or a press won't do.

*8.   *Scissors:* Small or large, you will need a pair of scissors to trim thread and cut miscellaneous papers.

*9.   *Bulldog clips:* Look through your office supplies to find a few of these handy clips. Use them to hold pages together while punching holes and binding.

*10.   *Paste brushes:* Paste or glue brushes are available as round or flat. They also come in a variety of sizes. Use a small brush to apply paste to small areas. Use a large brush to apply paste to larger surface areas and also for smoothing. All-purpose craft brushes are an inexpensive substitute and serve the same purpose.

*11.   *Self-healing cutting mat:* A surface to protect your table while cutting and punching holes is important. Cutting mats are available in a variety of sizes.

*12.   *Metal ruler:* Use this tool to measure and also as a guide for cutting straight lines with a craft knife. A cork backing is recommended to prevent slipping.

*13.   *Craft knife or utility knife:* Use a small craft knife to trim papers and book cloth. Use a utility knife to cut through book board, cardboard, and other thick materials. Always keep a sharp blade and use this tool on a protective surface.

*14.   *Awl:* The tip of this tool punches through thick stacks of paper while the handle protects your hand. Always use it on a protective surface. Awls are available in several sizes.

15.   *Hollow punch:* Use a heavy-duty hollow punch to create holes in book board and stacks of paper. Tap the tool with a hammer, and always use it on a protective surface. These punches often come in a variety of sizes.

16.   *Eyelet setter:* Change out the bits and some hollow punches double as an eyelet-setting punch. After punching a hole, tap this tool with a hammer to set an eyelet through the hole.

17.   *Japanese screw punch and bits:* A screw punch twists as you push it down to cut smoothly through paper, fabric, and leather. You can easily

punch through several layers of paper at a time but will find thick stacks of paper or book board challenging. Interchangeable bits come in a variety of sizes. Always use it on a protective surface.

18. *Single hole hand punch:* You will find this tool among office supplies. The standard hole size is ¼"; smaller hole sizes are also available.

19. *Hammer:* Use this tool with a hollow punch. It is also useful for setting snaps and jean rivets.

20. *Needle nose pliers:* A basic pair will assist you in pulling your needle and thread through thick stacks of paper. You can also use these pliers to work with wire.

21. *Hand drill:* This tool drills rough holes through book board and stacks of paper.

22. *Craft punch:* These punches are available in a variety of shapes and sizes. You may even find a punch that rounds the corners of pages. Use them to punch shapes from paper and thin card stock.

23. *Rotary perforator:* Use this tool to perforate paper. Always use it on a protective surface.

24. *Tape:* Use gentle removable tape to hold slippery materials in place when punching holes. Permanent double-sided tape can sometimes be used in place of paste or glue.

25. *Fabric pins:* Use these to hold pieces of fabric together.

26. *Fabric marking pencil:* Mark fabrics before sewing with this special pencil. The marks should easily brush or wash away after your project is complete.

27. *Fabric scissors or rotary cutter:* Both of these tools cleanly cut through fabric. Always use a rotary cutter on a protective surface.

28. *Iron:* Use a hot iron to press and smooth fabric. Set the temperature according to the manufacturer's recommendations for a particular type of fabric. Always use an iron on a protective surface, such as an ironing board.

29. *Ironing board:* Protect your table from the heat of an iron by using an ironing board.

30. *Sewing machine:* This tool quickly stitches pieces of fabric together. If you do not have a sewing machine, you can sew projects by hand with a needle and thread.

31. *Snap-setting tool:* Use this tool to set snaps in fabric. Many setting tools only work with specific sized snaps.

32. *Book press:* This tool provides pressure to flatten and smooth projects as they dry. You can easily substitute a heavy stack of books or a few bricks to press your projects instead.

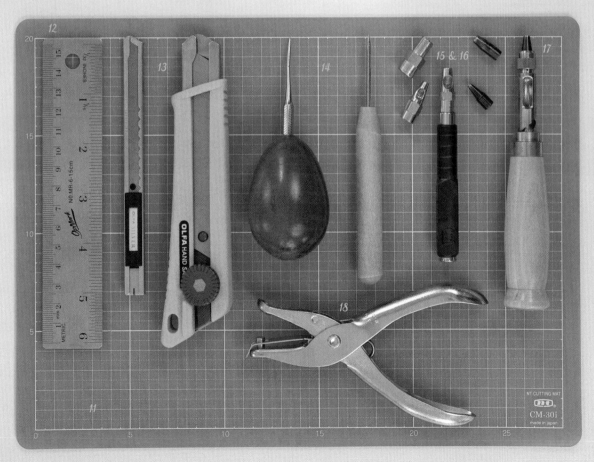

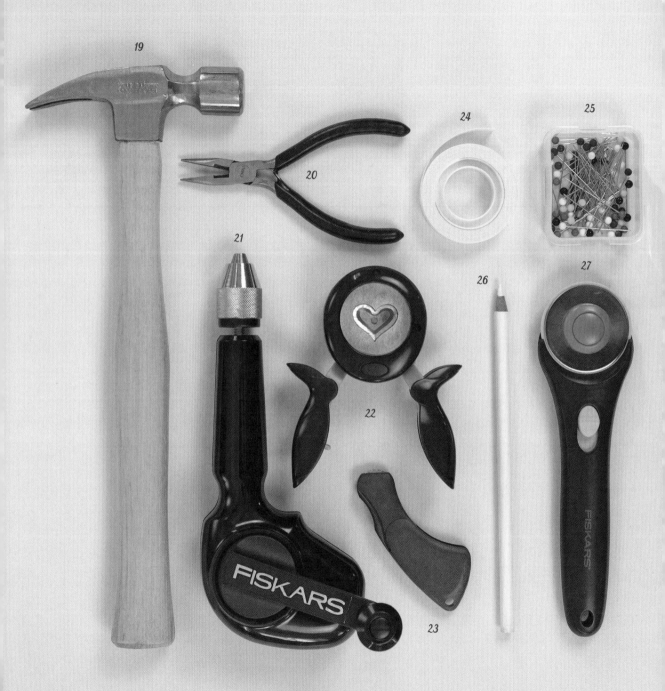

32

THREAD, RIBBON, CORD, AND STRING

There are limitless options available when choosing binding materials. Linen thread, known for its strength, is a standard among bookbinders. Many traditional Japanese books are bound with silk thread. Your local craft and sewing stores will carry a selection to choose from. Look for interesting options among the jewelry and sewing aisles.

1. Waxed linen thread

2. Unwaxed linen thread

3. Hemp cord

4. Cotton cord

5. Leather cord

6. Coated jewelry wire

7. Kitchen twine

8. Baker's twine

9. Metallic embroidery floss

10. Embroidery floss

11. Yarn

12. Fishing line

13. Ribbon

14. Twill tape

15. Baby rickrack

16. Elastic cord

PAPERS

Paper is available in all thicknesses, textures, and colors. Traditional Japanese bookbinding utilizes Japanese papers, which have a wonderful texture, strength, and flexibility to them. Western papers are a bit different from Japanese papers, but they can be used in many of the same ways. Remember to consider the direction of the grain when choosing papers for specific projects.

For the inside pages of your projects, you will use text weight paper, which is about the thickness of printer paper. For pages that will hold photos, try paper that is just a bit thicker than text weight paper, such as heavy weight drawing paper. Card stock is thicker yet and works well for small book covers. For hard book covers, begin with a core of bookbinder's board and cover it with decorative paper or book cloth.

Take the opportunity to be creative with your paper selections. Keep an eye out for interesting papers among things that you might normally throw away or recycle, such as food packaging and junk mail. Any of these examples of papers can be used for your book projects:

1. Japanese kozo paper
2. Ruled or gridded paper
3. Construction paper
4. Book cloth (learn how to make your own on pages 146–47)
5. Marbled paper
6. Magazine page
7. Book page
8. Mail packaging
9. Map
10. Ticket
11. Tea bag
12. Security envelope
13. Manila file folder
14. Hand-printed paper
15. Transparent paper
16. Wrapping paper
17. Calendar page
18. Origami
19. Paint chip
20. Packaging
21. Handmade paper
22. Brown kraft paper
23. Wallpaper
24. Printed music

Book cloth is a paper-backed cloth. It is a durable yet flexible material, perfect for hinges and the outside of book projects. It is often adhered to bookbinder's board to create hard covers. The paper backing prevents paste and glue from seeping through the back side of the cloth. Book cloth is often expensive and is limited to a small selection of colors and textures. If you make your own book cloth, you have a wide variety of fabrics to choose from.

Finished Size
Varies

Tools
Cutting mat or protective cutting surface
Spray bottle
Large stiff-bristle brush
Waxed paper
Paste or glue
Large stiff-bristle paste brush
Wet tape or masking tape

Materials
Medium weight woven fabric (not stretchy)
Light weight paper: 1" larger than the piece of fabric on all four sides

Instructions

1. Place the fabric face down on a cutting mat or protective surface. To remove wrinkles, lightly mist the back of the fabric with water. Use a large, stiff-bristle brush to gently brush out the wrinkles. Brush in the same direction as the grain of the fabric.

2. Lay the light weight paper on waxed paper. Apply a very thin layer of glue with another stiff-bristle brush, evenly, over the entire surface.

3. Pick up the light weight paper and lay it over the back of the fabric, glue-side down.

4. Gently use the large dry brush to smooth the paper over the fabric. Remove all wrinkles. Do not press too hard or the glue may soak through the front of the fabric.

5. Flip the paper-backed fabric over onto a piece of fiberboard, wooden board, or back onto the cutting mat. Tape it down around the edges.

6. Allow the book cloth to dry flat for twenty-four hours.

ADHESIVES

Although variations of cooked wheat paste are the primary adhesives of traditional Japanese bookbinding, you are welcome to use the adhesive with which you are most comfortable. Many options are available.

Wheat starch paste: This archival adhesive is sold in powder form. To use, add water and cook the mixture to the desired consistency (it should come with instructions). One of the benefits of using paste is that the adhesion is reversible: only water is needed to remove and repair the pasted portions. Wheat starch paste can be adjusted to any consistency, from watery to thick. The main drawback is that the wet paste can grow mold if you keep it around too long. Place it in the refrigerator to make it last longer. I often mix wheat starch paste with PVA for a smoother consistency. PVA is not reversible, so if you mix it, the paste will lose its archival quality.

PVA: Another name for white glue, this adhesive dries acid-free and is found almost anywhere. If it is too thick, add water to thin it, or mix it with prepared wheat starch paste. PVA creates a permanent bond. You may substitute other forms of white glue, such as school glue, for PVA. Remember that white glue that is not specifically labeled as PVA may contain additives and may not be acid-free.

Glue stick: A permanent, acid-free glue stick will often do the trick. Use it to paste small areas together. I do not recommend using a glue stick when covering book board or gluing large surfaces together.

Double-sided tape: Look for an artists' quality tape. Only use acid-free tape on important projects.

Bookbinding Basics

Before beginning the projects, you will need to learn just a few basics. You will notice several bookbinding terms used throughout the projects. These terms are explained in the Structure and Techniques sections. The stitches at the heart of Japanese bookbinding are included in the Stitching Techniques section (see pages 152–93).

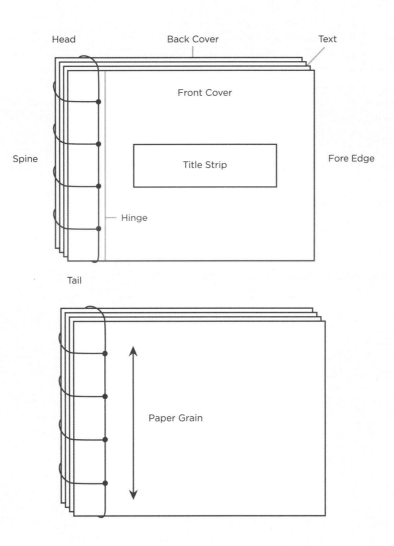

STRUCTURE

The following are common bookbinding terms. You will notice several of these terms used in the project instructions.

Book block: The stack of pages between the covers, sometimes referred to as "text."

Covers: Outer material that protects the inside pages. The front cover and the back cover sandwich the pages between them.

Endpaper: A decorative paper pasted to the inside of the front or back cover, or both.

Fore edge: The right edge of a book, opposite of the spine.

Head: The top edge of a book.

Hinge: A flexible fold in a cover that allows the cover to easily open and close.

Paper grain: The direction in which the fibers lie. It is important that the grain of the paper runs parallel to the spine. This allows the cover and pages to open easily. (See the Techniques section for ways to determine the direction of the paper grain.)

Spine: The left edge of a book, where the book is bound.

Tail: The bottom edge of a book, opposite of the head.

Text: The stack of pages between the covers, sometimes referred to as a "book block."

Title strip: A rectangular strip of paper pasted to the front cover, displaying the book's title.

TECHNIQUES

Most bookbinding techniques are fairly simple, but do be careful, especially when using sharp knives and awls. Always cut away from yourself; when you are stitching, pull your needle away from yourself. Keep a clean workspace, and protect your tabletop with a cutting mat when using sharp tools and waxed paper when using adhesives.

Burnish: To smooth a fold. Lay your paper on a flat surface and gently slide the long, flat side of a bone folder or wood tool along a folded edge.

Cut: To trim materials to desired size. You can use either scissors or a craft knife and metal ruler to cut your papers. When using a craft, or utility, knife, always cut on a protective surface. Use extra caution when cutting through book board and other thick materials. You will need to use a fresh blade and make several passes in order to cut all the way through.

Double knot: To tie an overhand knot in the same place, twice in a row.

Fold: To create a crease by bending one part of a paper over another part of itself. Whenever possible fold paper along the grain of the paper. This is particularly important with accordion books where the grain of the paper should run parallel to the fold.

You can use a couple of ways to discover the grain of your paper. If you tear a strip of paper along the grain, it will tear in a smooth, straight line. If you tear a strip of paper against the grain, it will tear in a jagged, irregular line. Another way to find the paper grain is to lay a sheet of paper flat on a table. Gently lift the right side over toward the left side (do not completely fold) and notice how flat the page lies. Try this again, bringing the top side over toward the bottom side. The page will be more flexible as you fold along with the grain. The page will be more resistant to folding against the grain.

Nest: To place one page into the fold of another. When working with projects that are folded along the spine, you will often nest the inside pages into the cover, placing the folded edge of the pages against the inside fold of the cover.

Paste or glue: To adhere papers. Always start with a fresh layer of waxed paper to protect your work surface. If you are using wet paste or glue to adhere papers together, apply a thin layer to one paper with a paste brush. Carefully lay the pasted page in place. In most cases you will smooth and press your pages after pasting. It is important to rinse your paste brush well, just after you use it.

Press: To apply pressure to a project. You can use either a book press or a heavy stack of books or bricks. Most often, you will press freshly pasted materials so that they dry completely flat. Sandwich your projects in clean waxed paper before pressing and allow them to dry completely before removing.

Punch: To create a hole in your paper. Several punching tools provide different hole sizes. Make a hole that accommodates the size of your thread or ribbon.

Score: To create a crease with a bone folder or other tool prior to folding. The best technique is to place a metal ruler on top of your paper where you want to create a score line. Slide the pointed end of a bone folder along the ruler, pressing down into the paper. Scoring does not cut through; it allows covers and pages to open more easily.

Smooth: To gently remove bubbles and wrinkles from freshly pasted papers. Use either a brush or the long, flat side of a bone folder or wood tool. Carefully smooth from the top side, moving your tool from the center toward the edges.

Thread a needle: To prepare a needle and thread for stitching. When stitching bookbinding projects, you will use a single thread. Take one end of the thread through the eye of a needle and pull about 4" of thread through. The longer portion of the thread is what you will use to bind your book.

Tie off: To tie the remaining threads together after binding to prevent the stitching from unraveling.

Stitching Techniques

The projects within this book are bound with traditional Japanese bindings or variations thereof. Most of the Japanese bindings are stab bindings. The covers are stitched to the pages through holes that penetrate all the way through the book from front to back. The best-known stab bindings include the Japanese four-hole binding, the noble binding, the hemp-leaf binding, and the tortoise-shell binding. These are often referred to as the four traditional Japanese stab bindings. Other stab bindings include the Yamato binding and the account book binding. You may experiment with any of these bindings and adjust the designs to your liking. The improvised Japanese four-hole binding is an example.

Apart from the accordions, the one Japanese binding included in this book that is not a stab binding is the ledger binding. This binding is sewn along the fold rather than stitched through the book from front to back.

The pages of traditional stab bindings are held together with a special inner binding within the covers. The inner binding remains in place, even after the covers are attached. The projects in this book are adapted for use with a basic bulldog clip instead of an inner binding. Use bulldog clips to temporarily hold together a project as you work. You may wish to use a clip at the fore edge of your book block to hold the pages together while you stitch. You may even use a clip on the outside of the cover if the materials that you are working with allow it. Always place a thick piece of paper underneath the clip to project your cover and pages from damage.

Each binding has its own traditional measurements, which are presented with the instructions for each stitch, for placement of the holes. From text weight or scrap paper, create a template paper the same size as the pages or cover of your book. Mark the holes on this template with a pencil and ruler, and use it as a guide to punch holes in the covers and pages. The measurements provided for each binding are just guidelines. Once you get the hang of the bindings, you can use the same ratios provided to make larger books. Experiment by adding more holes or placing them at different distances from the spine and from each other.

The amount of thread you will need varies for each project. The thickness of your pages, the distance of the holes from the spine, and the number of holes all affect the thread length. You will often use more thread than you think! (All of the projects in this book have a suggested thread length.) It is better to start with too much and trim the excess at the end. If you run short while stitching, take your needle through a hole in the cover and into the pages to tie on another length of thread. Leave the knot concealed between the pages and continue stitching from there.

Use a strong thread and pull it tight as you stitch. The larger the holes are in the cover and pages, the easier it is to pull the needle and thread through. Sometimes the needle may become difficult to pull through, especially when passing through the same hole several times. If this is the case, use a pair of pliers to grasp the end of the needle and pull it through. Be very careful to protect yourself and others when stitching. Always pull the needle away from yourself and others.

The Japanese four-hole binding is the most basic of the traditional Japanese stab bindings. It serves as the foundation for the other stab bindings.

1. This binding requires four holes. The standard alignment of the holes is ⅜" from the edge of the spine. Place the top hole ⅝" from the top edge of the book, place the bottom hole ⅝" from the bottom edge of the book, and place two more holes evenly between the first two holes. Mark the placement of each hole on a template paper cut to the same size as the top page or cover. You will use a length of thread five times the height of the spine.

2. You may leave a clip on the fore edge of your pages while you stitch, if you like. Place a small scrap of paper between the clip and your pages to prevent the clip from damaging your pages.

1a

3/8"

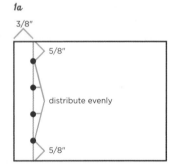

5/8"

distribute evenly

5/8"

1b

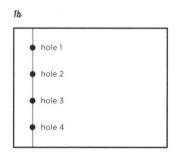

hole 1

hole 2

hole 3

hole 4

2

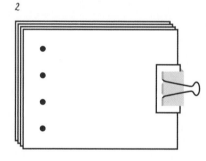

3. To begin, split apart your pages about halfway through the stack. Enter from the inside of the book through hole 2. Leave about 4" of thread inside the book. You will use this section of thread to tie off when you are finished stitching.

4. Place the pages back together in a stack and wrap your thread around the spine, entering hole 2 from back to front.

5. Proceed down the spine through hole 3 from front to back. Wrap the spine and enter hole 3 from front to back again. (Note: It may appear as though you are missing steps as you proceed down the spine. Don't worry; you will complete the missed areas as you work your way back up.)

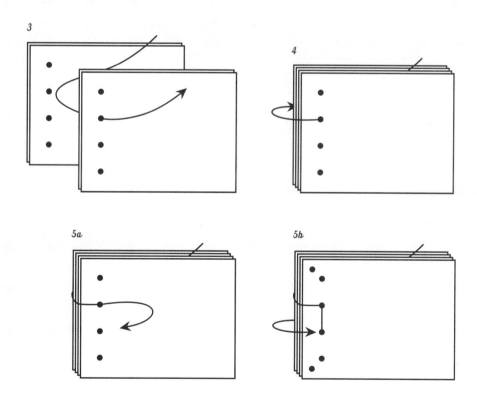

6. Enter hole 4 from back to front. Wrap the spine and enter hole 4 from back to front again. Then wrap the bottom of the book and enter through hole 4 back to front a third time.

7. Proceed up the spine through hole 3 from front to back, through hole 2 from back to front, and then through hole 1 from front to back.

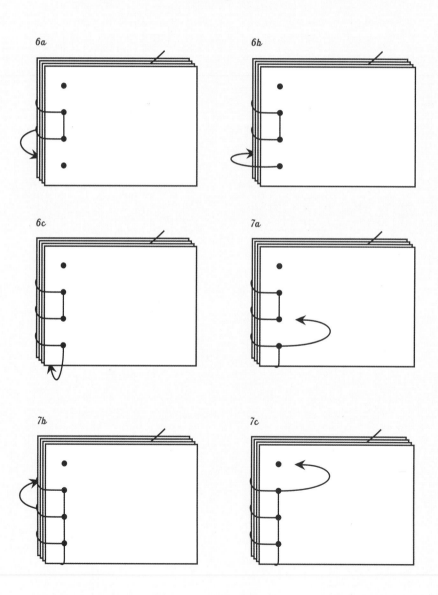

8. Wrap the spine and enter hole 1 from front to back. Then wrap the top of the book and enter hole 1 from front to back again.

9. At this point, you are almost finished. Remove the clip, if you are using one. Carefully proceed through hole 2 from the back to the inside of the book where you began.

10. Open up your pages to the two threads. Tie the threads in a tight double knot, right up against hole 2 where they came through. Trim the threads to about ½" and carefully tuck them back into the stitched spine, hiding them from view.

11. The completed Japanese four-hole binding.

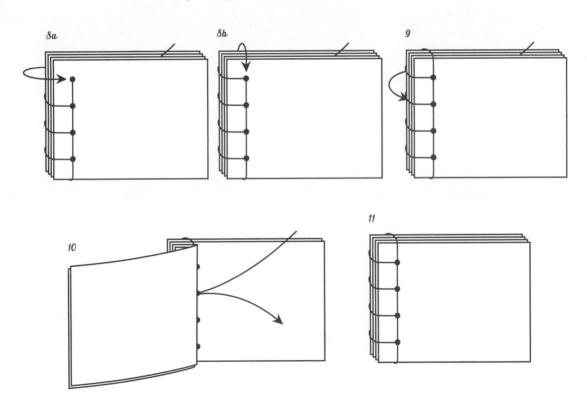

The noble binding is the same as the Japanese four-hole binding, with a little extra twist. The addition of decorative stitches strengthens the corners. This makes the noble binding a good choice for larger books.

1. This binding requires six holes. The standard alignment of the four main holes is ⅜" from the edge of the spine. Place the top hole ⅝" from the top edge of the book, place the bottom hole ⅝" from the bottom edge of the book, and place two more holes evenly between the first two holes. Holes 1a and 4b align ³⁄₁₆" from the edge of the spine (halfway between the row of four holes and the spine). Place hole 1a ⁵⁄₁₆" from the top edge of the book and place hole 4b ⁵⁄₁₆" from the bottom edge of the book. Mark the placement of each hole on a template paper cut to the same size as the top page or cover. You will use a length of thread six times the height of the spine.

2. You may leave a clip on the fore edge of your pages while you stitch, if you like. Place a small scrap of paper between the clip and your pages to prevent the clip from damaging your pages.

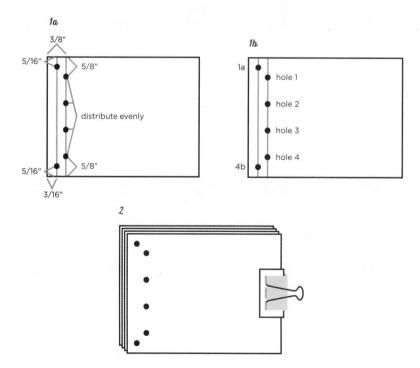

3. To begin, split apart your pages about halfway through the stack. Enter from the inside of the book through hole 2. Leave about 4" of thread inside the book. You will use this section of thread to tie off when you are finished stitching.

4. Place the pages back together in a stack and wrap your thread around the spine, entering hole 2 from back to front.

5. Proceed down the spine through hole 3 from front to back. Wrap the spine and enter hole 3 from front to back again. (Note: It may appear as though you are missing steps as you proceed down the spine. Don't worry; you will complete the missed areas as you work your way back up.)

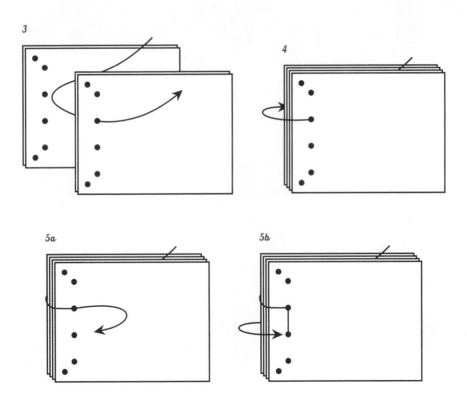

6. Enter hole 4 from back to front. Wrap the spine and enter hole 4 from back to front again. Then wrap the bottom of the book and enter through hole 4 back to front a third time.

7. At this point, enter hole 4b from front to back. Wrap the spine and enter hole 4b front to back again.

8. Wrap the bottom of the book and enter 4b front to back for a third time.

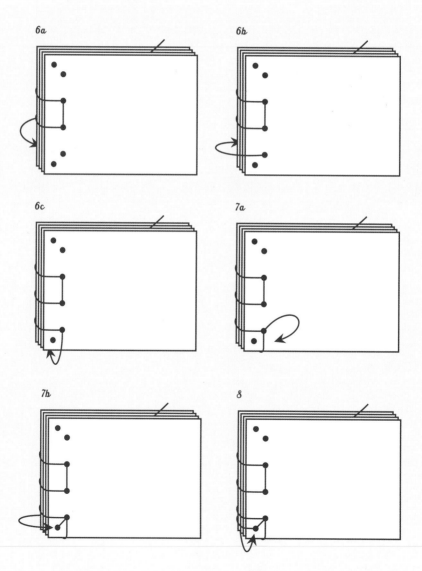

6a   6b

6c   7a

7b   8

9. Complete the corner by entering hole 4 from back to front.

10. Proceed up the spine through hole 3 from front to back, through hole 2 from back to front, and then through hole 1 from front to back.

11. Wrap the spine and enter hole 1 from front to back again. Then wrap the top of the book and enter hole 1 from front to back a third time.

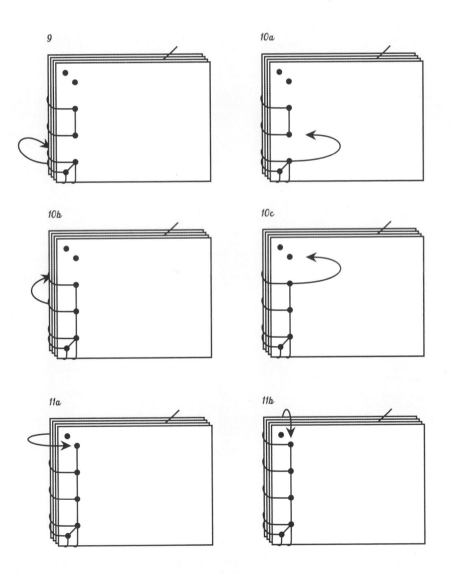

12. Enter hole 1a from back to front. Wrap the spine and enter hole 1a from back to front again.

13. Wrap the top of the book and enter hole 1a back to front a third time.

14. Complete the top corner by entering hole 1 from front to back.

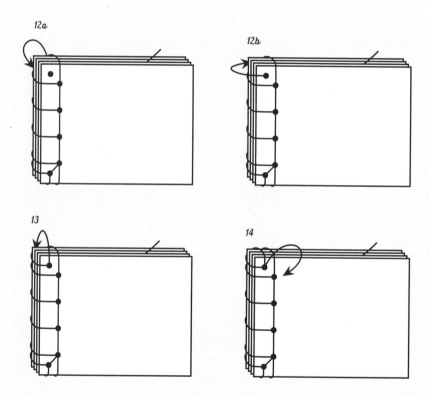

15. At this point you are almost finished. Remove the clip, if you are using one. Carefully proceed through hole 2 from the back to the inside of the book where you began.

16. Open up your pages to the two threads. Tie the threads in a tight double knot, right up against hole 2 where they came through. Trim the threads to about ½" and carefully tuck them back into the stitched spine, hiding them from view.

17. The completed noble binding.

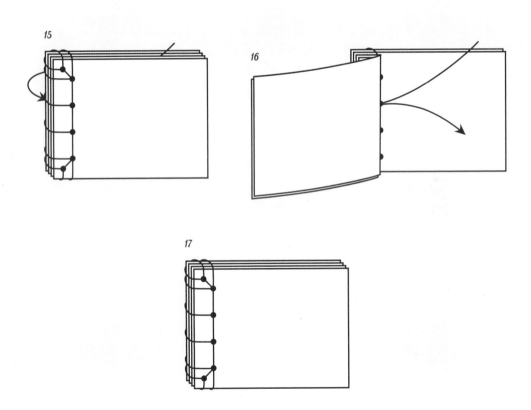

The hemp-leaf binding is another step past the noble binding in complexity. It too begins in the same way as the Japanese four-hole binding. The decorative stitches, which resemble the shape of a hemp leaf, build on the stitching pattern found at the corners of the noble binding. The additional stitches strengthen the spine, making the hemp-leaf binding another good choice for larger books.

1. This binding requires nine holes. The standard alignment of the four main holes is ⅜" from the edge of the spine. Place the top hole ⅝" from the top edge of the book, place the bottom hole ⅝" from the bottom edge of the book, and place two more holes evenly between the first two holes. The five secondary holes align ³⁄₁₆" from the edge of the spine (halfway between the row of four holes and the spine). Place hole 1a halfway between the top edge of the book and hole 1. Place hole 2a halfway between hole 1 and hole 2. Place hole 3a halfway between hole 2 and 3. Place hole 4a halfway between hole 3 and hole 4. Place hole 4b halfway between hole 4 and the bottom edge of the book. Mark the placement of each hole on a template paper cut to the same size as the top page or cover. You will use a length of thread eight times the height of the spine.

2. You may leave a clip on the fore edge of your pages while you stitch, if you like. Place a small scrap of paper between the clip and your pages to prevent the clip from damaging your pages.

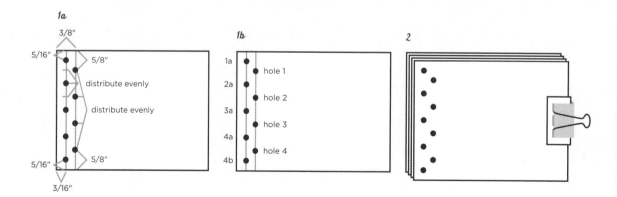

3. To begin, split apart your pages about halfway through the stack. Enter from the inside of the book through hole 2. Leave about 4" of thread inside the book. You will use this section of thread to tie off when you are finished stitching.

4. Place the pages back together in a stack and wrap your thread around the spine, entering hole 2 from back to front.

5. Proceed down the spine through hole 3 from front to back. Wrap the spine and enter hole 3 from front to back again. (Note: It may appear as though you are missing steps as you proceed down the spine. Don't worry; you will complete the missed areas as you work your way back up.)

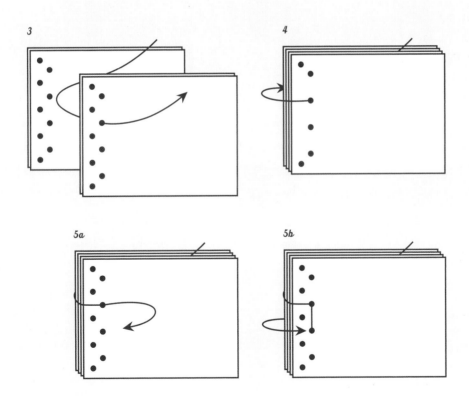

6. Enter hole 4 from back to front. Wrap the spine and enter hole 4 from back to front again. Then wrap the bottom of the book and enter through hole 4 back to front a third time.

7. At this point, enter hole 4b from front to back. Wrap the spine and enter hole 4b front to back again.

8. Wrap the bottom of the book and enter hole 4b front to back a third time.

9. Complete the corner by entering hole 4 from back to front.

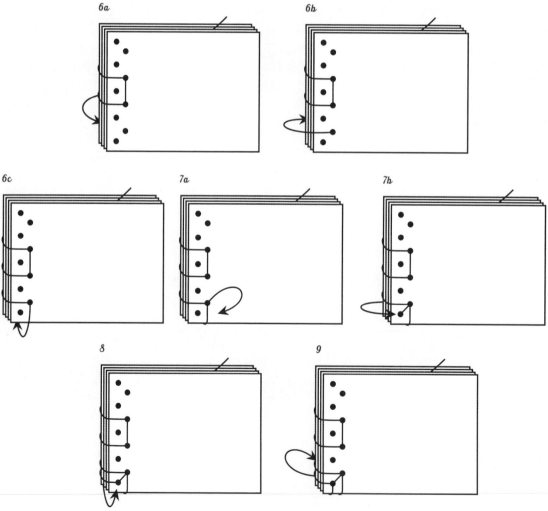

10. Proceed up the spine through hole 4a from front to back.

11. Wrap the spine and enter hole 4a from front to back again.

12. Go down the spine into hole 4 from back to front.

13. Proceed up the spine through hole 3 from front to back.

14. Go down the spine through hole 4a from back to front, then back up the spine through hole 3 from front to back.

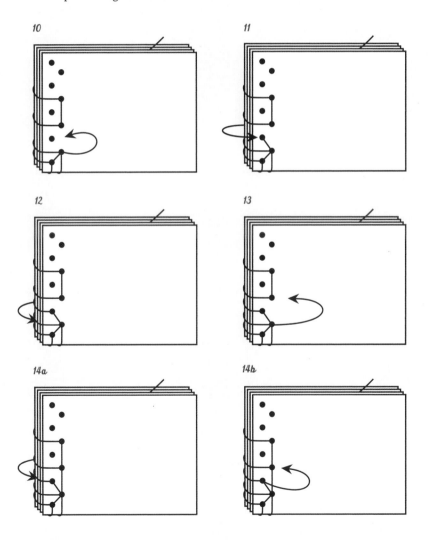

15. Enter hole 3a from back to front. Wrap the spine and enter hole 3a from back to front again.

16. Go down the spine through hole 3 from front to back.

17. Proceed up the spine through hole 2 from back to front.

18. Go down the spine through hole 3a from front to back and proceed up the spine through hole 2 back to front.

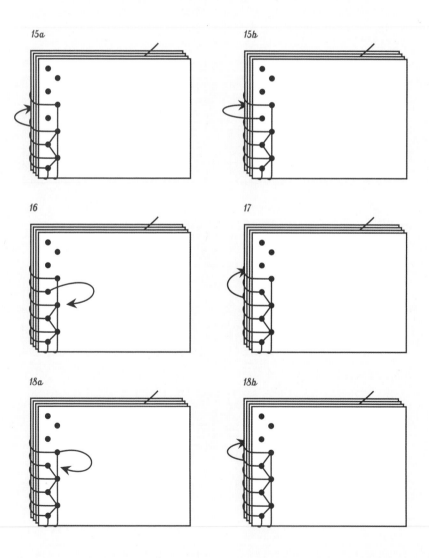

19. Proceed up the spine through hole 1 from front to back.

20. Wrap the spine and enter hole 1 from front to back again. Then wrap the top of the book and enter hole 1 from front to back a third time.

21. Enter hole 1a from back to front. Wrap the spine and enter hole 1a back to front again.

22. Wrap the top of the book and enter hole 1a back to front a third time.

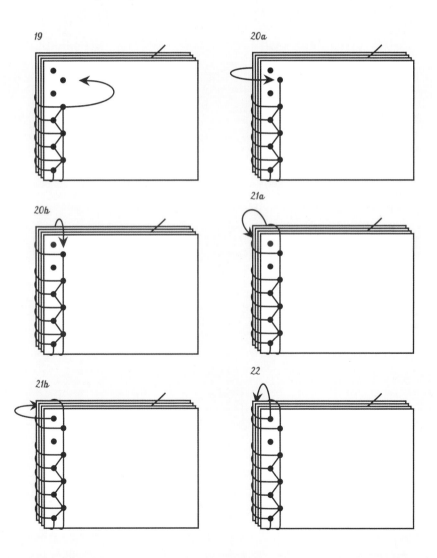

23. Complete the corner by entering hole 1 from front to back.

24. Go down the spine through hole 2a from back to front. Wrap the spine and enter hole 2a from back to front again.

25. Go down the spine through hole 2 from front to back, then proceed up the spine through hole 2a from back to front.

26. Proceed up the spine through hole 1 from front to back.

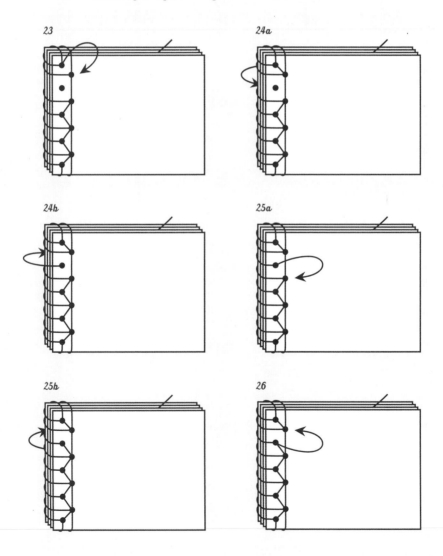

27. At this point you are almost finished. Remove the clip, if you are using one. Carefully proceed through hole 2 from the back to the inside of the book where you began.

28. Open up your pages to the two threads. Tie the threads in a tight double knot, right up against hole 2 where they came through. Trim the threads to about ½" and carefully tuck them back into the stitched spine, hiding them from view.

29. The completed hemp-leaf binding.

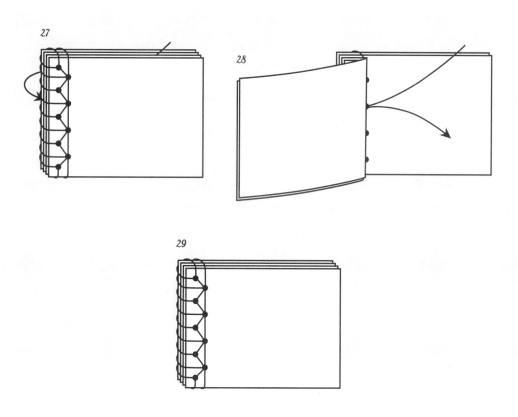

The tortoise-shell binding is slightly different in appearance from the other stab bindings, although it does begin in the same way as the Japanese four-hole binding. The stitching pattern does not enclose the corners of the book like the noble and hemp-leaf bindings. Instead, it adds to the basic pattern of the Japanese four-hole binding, creating a design similar to the geometric pattern found on tortoise shells.

1. This binding requires twelve holes. The standard alignment of the four main holes is ⅜" from the edge of the spine. Place the top hole ⅝" from the top edge of the book, place the bottom hole ⅝" from the bottom edge of the book, and place two more holes evenly between the first two holes. The eight secondary holes align ³/₁₆" from the edge of the spine (halfway between the row of four holes and the spine). Place a hole ¼" above and below each main hole. Mark the placement of each hole on a template paper cut to the same size as the top page or cover. You will use a length of thread seven times the height of the spine.

2. You may leave a clip on the fore edge of your pages while you stitch, if you like. Place a small scrap of paper between the clip and your pages to prevent the clip from damaging your pages.

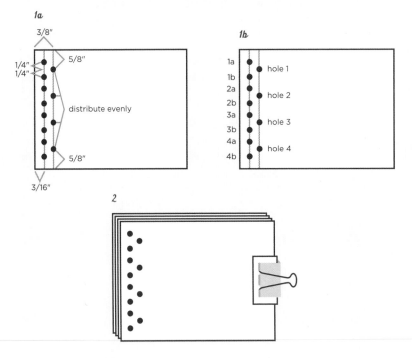

3. To begin, split apart your pages about halfway through the stack. Enter from the inside of the book through hole 2. Leave about 4" of thread inside the book. You will use this section of thread to tie off when you are finished stitching.

4. Place the pages back together in a stack and wrap your thread around the spine, entering hole 2 from back to front.

5. Proceed down the spine through hole 3 from front to back. Wrap the spine and enter hole 3 from front to back again. (Note: It may appear as though you are missing steps as you proceed down the spine. Don't worry; you will complete the missed areas as you work your way back up.)

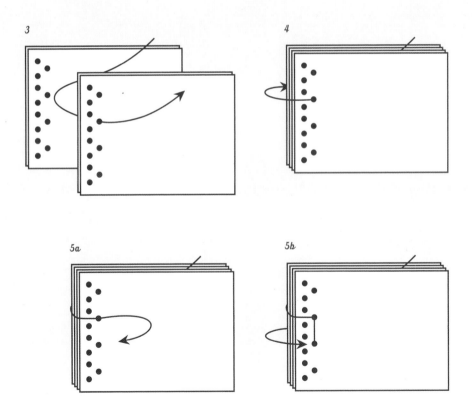

6. Enter hole 4 from back to front. Wrap the spine and enter hole 4 from back to front again. Then wrap the bottom of the book and enter through hole 4 back to front a third time.

7. From here, enter hole 4b from front to back. Wrap the spine and enter hole 4b from front to back again. Then enter hole 4 from back to front.

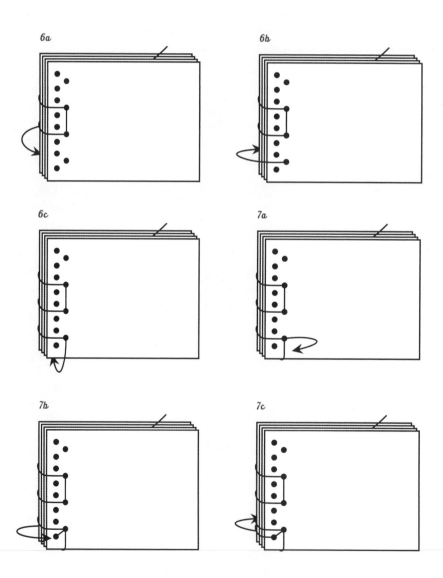

8.   Proceed up the spine through hole 4a from front to back. Wrap the spine and enter hole 4a from front to back again. Then go back down the spine through hole 4 from back to front.

9.   Proceed up the spine through hole 3 from front to back.

10. Imitate the pattern created through the previous two steps by going down the spine through hole 3b from back to front. Wrap the spine and enter hole 3b from back to front again. Then go back up the spine through hole 3 from front to back.

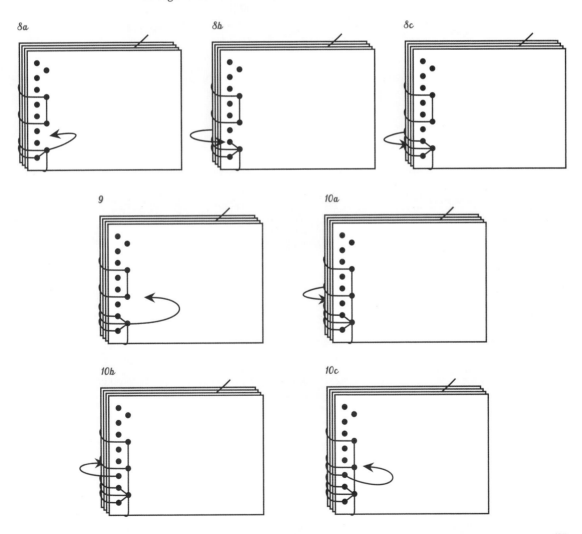

11. Proceed up the spine through hole 3a from back to front. Wrap the spine and enter hole 3a from back to front again. Then go back down the spine through hole 3 from front to back.

12. Proceed up through hole 2 from back to front.

13. Go down the spine through hole 2b from front to back. Wrap the spine and enter hole 2b from front to back again. Then go back up the spine through hole 2 from back to front.

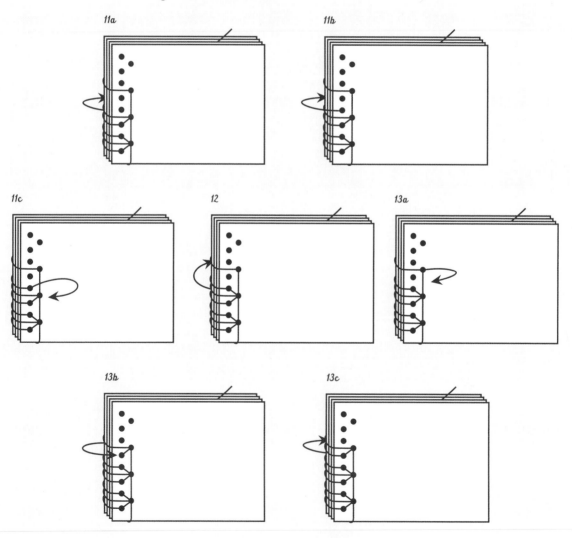

Stitching Techniques

14. Enter hole 2a from front to back. Wrap the spine and enter hole 2a from front to back again. Then go back down the spine through hole 2 from back to front.

15. Proceed up the spine through hole 1 from front to back.

16. Wrap the spine and enter hole 1 from front to back again. Then wrap the top of the book and enter hole 1 from front to back a third time.

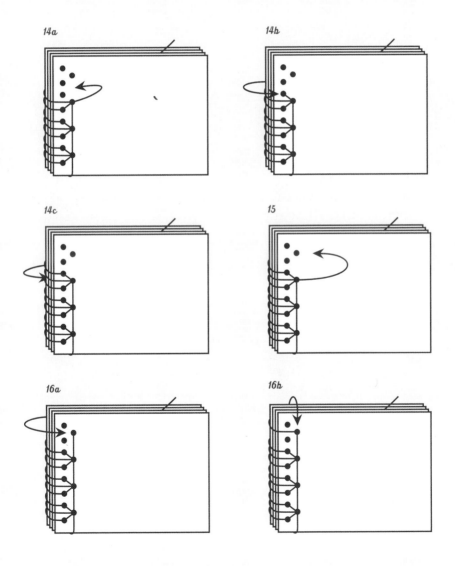

17. Enter hole 1a from back to front. Wrap the spine and enter hole 1a from back to front again. Then go back down the spine through hole 1 from front to back.

18. Go down the spine through hole 1b from back to front. Wrap the spine and enter hole 1b from back to front again. Then go back up the spine through hole 1 from front to back.

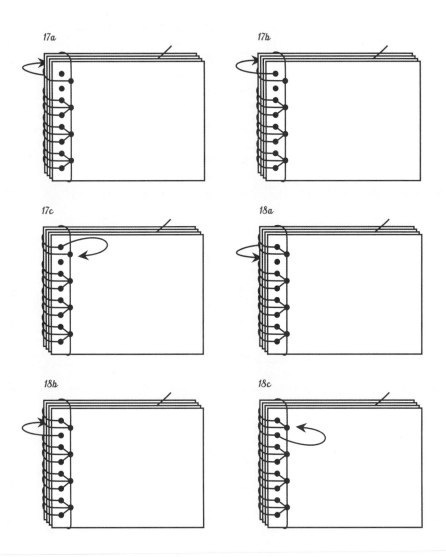

19. At this point you are almost finished. Remove the clip, if you are using one. Carefully proceed through hole 2 from the back to the inside of the book where you began.

20. Open up your pages to the two threads. Tie the threads in a tight double knot, right up against hole 2 where they came through. Trim the threads to about ½" and carefully tuck them back into the stitched spine, hiding them from view.

21. The completed tortoise-shell binding.

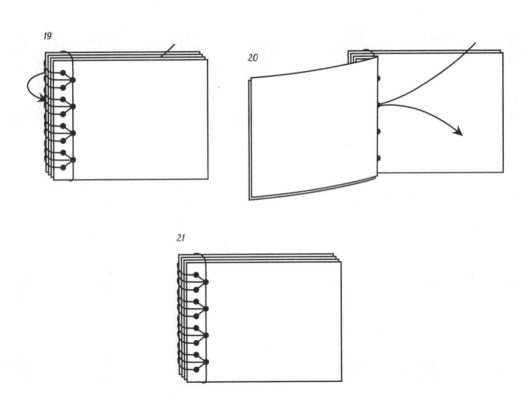

Although this is not one of the four traditional Japanese stab bindings, it begins in the same way as the Japanese four-hole binding. The thread wraps around the spine from one hole to the next to add an extra layer of interest.

1. This binding requires four holes. The standard alignment of the holes is ⅜" from the edge of the spine. Place the top hole ⅝" from the top edge of the book, place the bottom hole ⅝" from the bottom edge of the book, and place two more holes evenly between the first two holes. Mark the placement of each hole on a template paper cut to the same size as the top page or cover. You will use a length of thread seven times the height of the spine.

2. You may leave a clip on the fore edge of your pages while you stitch, if you like. Place a small scrap of paper between the clip and your pages to prevent the clip from damaging your pages.

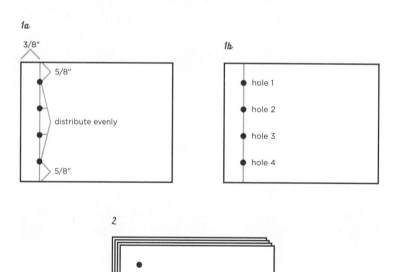

3. To begin, split apart your pages about halfway through the stack. Enter from the inside of the book through hole 2. Leave about 4" of thread inside the book. You will use this section of thread to tie off when you are finished stitching.

4. Place the pages back together in a stack and wrap your thread around the spine, entering hole 2 from back to front.

5. Proceed down the spine through hole 3 from front to back. Wrap the spine and enter hole 3 from front to back again. (Note: It may appear as though you are missing steps as you proceed down the spine. Don't worry; you will complete the missed areas as you work your way back up.)

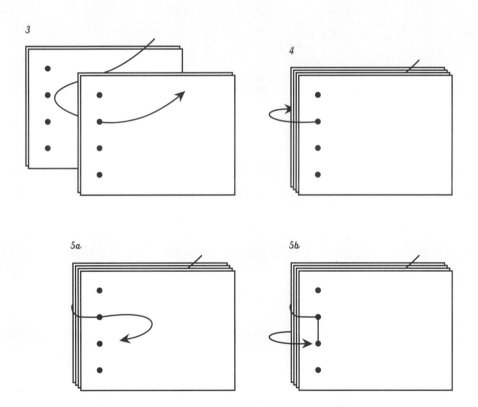

6. Enter hole 4 from back to front. Wrap the spine and enter hole 4 from back to front again. Then wrap the bottom of the book and enter through hole 4 back to front a third time.

7. Proceed up the spine through hole 3 from front to back, through hole 2 from back to front, and then through hole 1 from front to back.

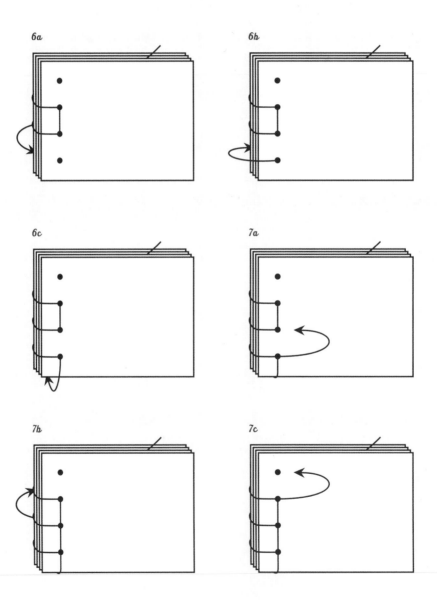

6a

6b

6c

7a

7b

7c

8.   Wrap the spine and enter hole 1 from front to back. Then wrap the top of the book and enter hole 1 from front to back again.

9.   Proceed down the spine through hole 2 from back to front.

10.   Wrap around and down the spine. Enter hole 3 from back to front.

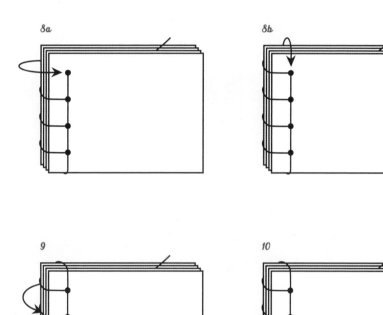

11. Wrap around and down the spine. Enter hole 4 from back to front.

12. Wrap around and up the spine. Enter hole 3 from back to front.

13. Wrap around and up the spine. Enter hole 2 from back to front.

14. Wrap around and up the spine. Enter hole 1 from back to front.

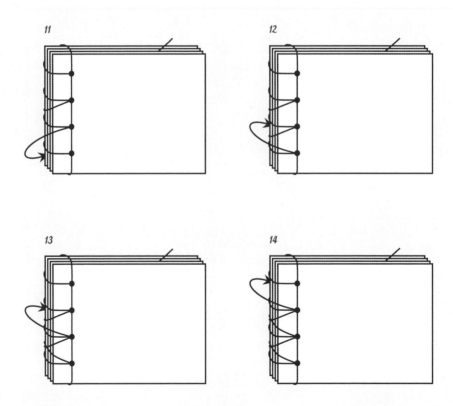

15. Wrap around and down the spine toward hole 2. At this point you are almost finished. Remove the clip, if you are using one. Carefully proceed through hole 2 from the back to the inside of the book where you began.

16. Open up your pages to the two threads. Tie the threads in a tight double knot, right up against hole 2 where they came through. Trim the threads to about ½" and carefully tuck them back into the stitched spine, hiding them from view.

17. The completed improvised Japanese four-hole binding.

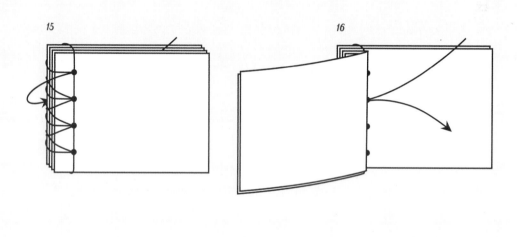

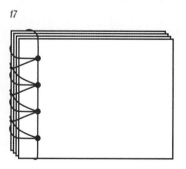

The Yamato binding is the simplest of all the stab bindings. It requires only two holes, and the threads tie at the outside of the cover. This binding is great for simple projects with few pages. Because the Yamato binding only requires two holes, you can easily use ribbon or even thin strips of folded paper to bind the pages together.

1. This binding requires two holes. The standard alignment of the holes is ½" from the edge of the spine. Divide the length of the spine into three parts. Place the holes at the two points dividing the three parts, evenly distributing the two holes between the top and bottom of the page. Mark the placement of each hole on a template paper cut to the same size as the top page or cover. You will use a length of thread three times the height of the spine.

2. You may leave a clip on the fore edge of your pages while you stitch, if you like. Place a small scrap of paper between the clip and your pages to prevent the clip from damaging your pages.

3. To begin, enter from the outside of the front cover through hole 1. Leave about half of the thread at the front of the book. You will use this section of thread to tie off when you are finished stitching.

4. Enter hole 2 from back to front.

5. Tie the threads in a tight double knot centered between the holes. Tie a bow, and trim the extra thread. The completed Yamato binding.

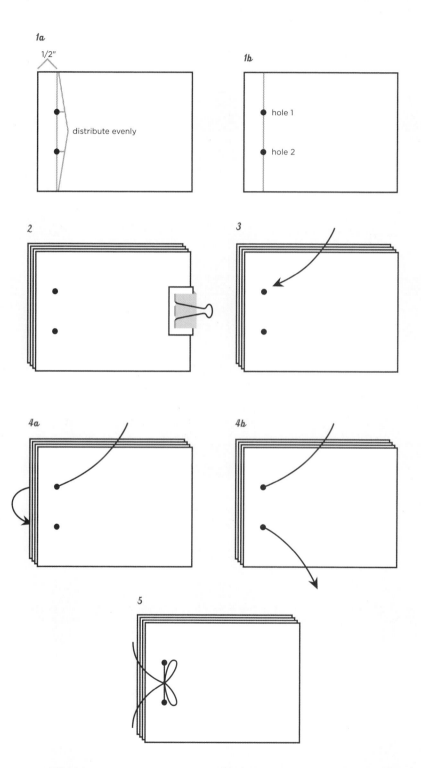

The account book binding is another simple stab binding. It is traditionally considered a type of ledger rather than a stab binding. This has more to do with the intended function than the stitching, which penetrates all the way through the book as the other stab bindings do. Throughout history, account books held important accounting information and could be tossed into a well at the threat of fire. The long threads extending from the top of the book made fetching them afterward a cinch. Nowadays, the threads at the top make the account book a great binding for books that hang.

1. This binding requires two holes. The standard alignment of the holes is ½" from the edge of the spine. Divide the length of the spine into three parts. Place the holes at the two points dividing the three parts, evenly distributing the two holes between the top and bottom of the page. Mark the placement of each hole on a template paper cut to the same size as the top page or cover. You will use two separate threads, one for each hole. Cut each thread to five times the height of the spine.

2. You may leave a clip on the fore edge of your pages while you stitch, if you like. Place a small scrap of paper between the clip and your pages to prevent the clip from damaging your pages.

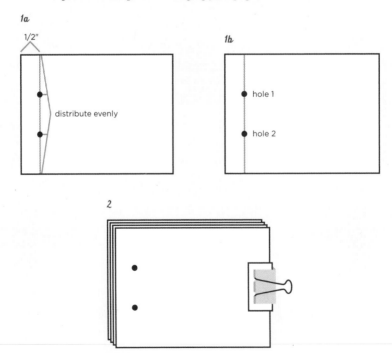

1a

1/2"

distribute evenly

1b

hole 1

hole 2

2

3. To begin, enter from the outside of the front cover through hole 1. Leave about one third of the thread at the front of the book. You will use this section of thread to tie off when you are finished stitching.

4. Wrap the top of the book and enter hole 1 from front to back again.

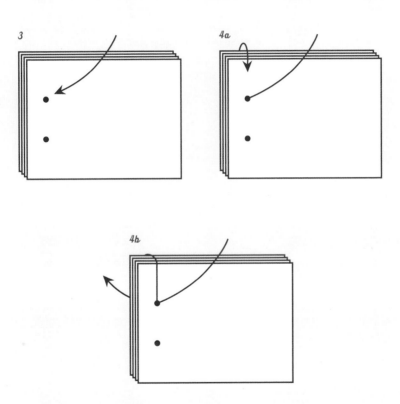

5. Tie the ends of the thread in a tight double knot centered over the spine and directly across from hole 1.

6. With the second thread, enter from the outside of the front cover through hole 2. Leave about one third of the thread at the front of the book to tie off.

5

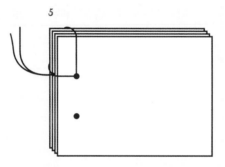

6

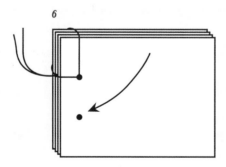

7. Wrap the bottom of the book and enter hole 2 from front to back again.

8. Tie the ends of the thread in a tight double knot centered over the spine and directly across from hole 2.

9. Twist each pair of threads tightly together. Tie the pairs of twisted threads together in a double knot centered over the spine and directly between the holes. Trim extra thread to a desired length. The completed account book binding.

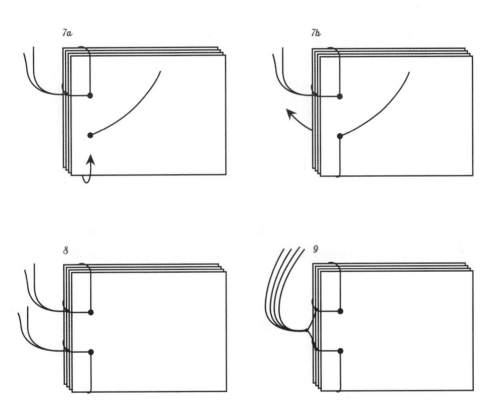

The ledger is technically a type of book rather than a binding. Ledgers are traditionally used as account books and receipt books, although they also make great memo pads and notebooks. The ledger illustrated here uses pages that are folded in half. The binding is sewn along the fold at the spine. The sewing pattern is identical to that of the pamphlet binding, a popular Western binding.

1. This binding requires three holes. The standard alignment of the holes is right along the edge of the spine. Place hole 2 directly in the center of the spine. Center hole 1 between hole 2 and the top of the page. Center hole 3 between hole 2 and the bottom of the page. Mark the placement of each hole on a template paper cut to the same size as the inside pages. You will use a length of thread three times the height of the spine.

2. To begin, enter from the outside of the spine through hole 2 to the inside of the book. Leave about one third of the thread at the outside of the book. You will use this section of thread to tie off when you are finished sewing.

3. Travel up along the inside of the book along the fold and exit at hole 1. Go down the outside of the spine and enter hole 3 to the inside of the book.

4. Travel up along the inside of the book along the fold and exit at hole 2.

5. Make sure each end of the thread is on opposite sides of the thread that runs along the spine. Tie the threads in a double knot centered over hole 2, securing the thread that runs along the spine in the knot. Trim the extra thread to desired length. The completed ledger binding.

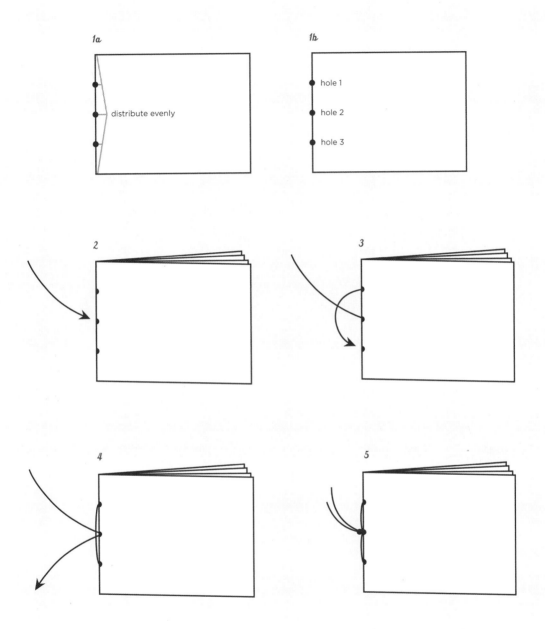

Resources

You will find many basic tools and supplies at your local arts and crafts store, office supply store, and hardware store. To find particular bookbinding tools and supplies, take a look at some of these online sources:

Blick Art Materials
www.dickblick.com
A great resource for all art materials, Blick carries basic bookbinding tools and other art tools that work well for bookbinding.

Hiromi Paper Inc.
www.hiromipaper.com
This Santa Monica–based business carries a large selection of Japanese and specialty papers as well as traditional Japanese bookbinding tools.

Hollander's
www.hollanders.com
This store offers a large selection of specialty papers. You will also find all types of bookbinding tools and supplies.

Jo-Ann Fabrics and Crafts
www.joann.com
Jo-Ann carries a wide variety of fabric and sewing notions. You can also find basic craft and scrapbooking tools. This is another great source for interesting string, ribbon, and embellishments.

Michaels
www.michaels.com
Michaels carries many basic craft and scrapbooking tools that work well for bookbinding. Keep an eye out for interesting string, ribbon, and embellishments.

Ofla
www.olfa.com
Here you will find the perfect cutting tools for any project.

Paper Source
www.paper-source.com
Look here for a fun selection of contemporary papers and basic bookbinding tools.

Royalwood Ltd.
www.royalwoodltd.com
This online source is one of the best for waxed linen thread at great prices.

Talas
www.talasonline.com
Here you will find specialty bookbinding and conservation materials that you cannot find elsewhere.

Utrecht Art Supplies
www.utrechtart.com
Utrecht is another great resource for all art materials as well as a few basic bookbinding tools.

These books are great resources for digging deeper into the nitty-gritty details of bookbinding:

Japanese Bookbinding: Instructions from a Master Craftsman
Kojiro Ikegami
Boston: Weatherhill, 2003

Non-Adhesive Binding: Books without Paste or Glue
Keith A. Smith
Rochester, N.Y.: Keith Smith, 2003

About the Author

Erin Zamrzla has loved making things from paper for as long as she can remember. As a design student, she took her first bookbinding class and thus began a wonderful adventure. She currently designs, teaches, and binds books in California. See more of her work at erinzam.com.